PAY AT THE CROSSROADS

Helen Murlis is a leading UK remuneration specialist and head of central government and agency consultancy at Hay Management Consultants. She joined Hay in 1990 and became a senior director in 1993. After early personnel management experience in the aerospace industry she worked for the British Institute of Management, first in research and then as executive remuneration adviser. She was the first head of IDS Top Pay Unit (now the Management Pay Review), following this with five years' consultancy experience at KPMG. Her expertise and consulting contribution cover both reward and performance management policy and practice, linked to human resource strategy development. As well as conducting reward strategy reviews both in the public and private sectors, she writes, lectures and broadcasts on a wide range of pay and performance management issues. She has contributed many articles to IPD publications, including *People Management*. She is co-author of two books: *Reward Management* (with Michael Armstrong) and *Jobs, Roles and People* (with Derek Pritchard). Between 1992 and 1994, when the discussions that launched this book began, she was IPM Vice President – Pay and Employment Conditions. She is also a founder member and past chairman of the IPD Compensation Forum.

The Institute of Personnel and Development is the leading publisher of books and reports for personnel and training professionals and students and for all those concerned with the effective management and development of people at work. For full details of all our titles please telephone the Publishing Department on 0181 263 3387.

PAY
AT THE CROSSROADS

Edited by
Helen Murlis

INSTITUTE OF PERSONNEL AND DEVELOPMENT

© Institute of Personnel and Development 1996

First published in 1996

All rights reserved. No part of this publication may be reproduced, stored in an information storage and retrieval system, or transmitted in any form or by any means, electronic, mechanical, photocopying, recording or otherwise, without the written permission of the Institute of Personnel and Development, IPD House, Camp Road, London, SW19 4UX.

Typeset by The Comp-Room, Aylesbury
Printed in Great Britain by
Short Run Press, Exeter

British Library Cataloguing-in-Publication Data

A catalogue record for this book is available from the British Library

ISBN 0-85292-614-6

The views expressed in this book are the authors' own, and may not necessarily reflect those of the IPD.

**INSTITUTE OF PERSONNEL
AND DEVELOPMENT**

IPD House, Camp Road, London SW19 4UX
Tel: 0181 971 9000   Fax: 0181 263 3333
Registered office as above. Registered Charity No. 1038333
A company limited by guarantee. Registered in England No. 2931892

Contents

Contributors	vi
Acknowledgements	x
1 • **Pay and the Business Agenda** *Stephen Palmer*	1
2 • **Pay at the Crossroads** *John Stevens*	24
3 • **How Do We Think about Pay?** *Ken Mayhew, Peter Ingram and David Guest*	39
4 • **The State of the Art in the Private Sector** *Clive Wright* ICL PLC– Mercury Communications – First Direct – Rover Group	57
5 • **The State of the Art in the Public Sector** *Robert Elliott and Helen Murlis* The Civil Aviation Authority – The Employment Service Agency – Derby City General Hospital – HM Customs & Excise	97
6 • **Managing the Paradoxes** *Helen Murlis*	138
References	153
Index	154

Contributors

Robert Elliott is a Professor of Economics at the University of Aberdeen. He was previously a lecturer at the University of Aberdeen and visiting professor at the Universities of Cornell, Stanford, and New York in the USA, at the University of Queensland in Australia, and at the Université Panthéon-Assas, Paris II. He is currently director of the Scottish Doctoral Programme in Economics. He has acted as consultant to the Bureau of Labour Market Research, the research arm of the Australian Department of Employment and Industrial Relations; to the Committee of Inquiry into Civil Service Pay; to Chairman Sir John Megaw; to the Police Federation of England and Wales; to HM Treasury; to OECD Paris; and to the European Commission. He has directed a large number of research projects in labour economics. He currently directs three research projects funded by the Leverhulme Trust, HM Treasury, and the Department of Education and Employment. He has published extensively in the field of labour economics in the *Economic Journal*, *Economica*, *The British Journal of Industrial Relations*, *The Bulletin of the Oxford Institute of Statistics*, *The Scottish Journal of Political Economy*, *Regional Studies*, *Urban Studies*, and *The Cambridge Journal of Economics*. Among his most recent books are *Labour Economics: A comparative text*, and *Unemployment and Labour Market Efficiency*.

David Guest obtained a first in psychology and sociology at Birmingham University. After postgraduate research, he became research officer in the Department of Occupational Psychology, Birkbeck College. He spent three years as behavioural science adviser to British Rail before joining the London School of Economics in 1972. He moved to Birkbeck in 1990. He has written and researched extensively in the areas of human resource management (HRM), and organisational commitment and change. He has worked closely with a range of organisations including, in recent years, Shell, ICL UK, IBM, BAT Industries, Hong Kong MTRC, Sanders and Sidney, the NHS, and British Rail. Current research interests cover HRM on greenfield sites, employee commitment and new forms of contract, the future of the career, and evaluation of culture change. He is currently joint editor of *The British Journal of Industrial Relations*.

Peter Ingram works in the Department of Economics, the University of Surrey, and is a member of the industrial relations programme at the Centre for Economic Performance at the London School of Economics. His current research is financed by the Leverhulme Trust. He has published on issues related to pay determination, productivity, and industrial relations.

Ken Mayhew is Fellow and Tutor in Economics at Pembroke College, Oxford. He was educated at Worcester College, Oxford (MA in Modern History) and at the London School of Economics (MSc in Economics). His previous employers include HM Treasury and the Oxford University Institute of Economics and Statistics. In 1989 and 1990 he was economic director of the National Economic Development Office. He has researched and published widely on labour market issues both in Britain and abroad. Much of his recent research (in collaboration with Ewart Keep of Warwick Business School) has been concerned with vocational education and training. He has acted as consultant to many UK and foreign organisations. Currently he is an associate editor of the *Oxford Review of Economic Policy*. His main administrative duties are as chairman of the Committee for the Oxford University Management School, and as Tutor for Admissions at Pembroke College. Among his recent publications are *Britain's Trading Deficit* (edited with Richard Layard and Geoffrey Owen) and *Improving Health Care* (edited with Paul Fenn and Alistair McGuire).

Stephen Palmer began his industrial relations career as assistant research officer with the National Union of Seamen. He left to study for a master's degree at the London School of Economics, and later joined Incomes Data Services as a senior researcher on pay and conditions. In 1979 he started at the (then) Institute of Personnel Management as policy adviser on pay and employment conditions, a post he held for 11 years before becoming the Institute's Assistant Director – Development. In 1992 he was appointed deputy director of employment affairs with the Confederation of British Industry. He is now remuneration adviser at the Office of Manpower Economics. He lives in South London with his wife and two cats. He is also a lifelong supporter of Wolverhampton Wanderers FC and Leicestershire County Cricket Club, and is therefore no stranger to adversity.

John Stevens first worked in the chemical industry, particularly on herbicide development. Having studied for HND in Business Studies at the City of London College, he then worked in the economic department of the Trades Union Congress (TUC), particularly on collective bargaining and pay policy, but he was also responsible for a range of industry topics such as accountancy and insolvency. He joined the National Economic Development Office in 1978 and, after a spell in the Industry Division, moved to the Manpower Division, becoming responsible for manpower work on the engineering industry, particularly on electrical power engineering and manufacturing systems engineering. He developed joint NEDO/Employment Department work on human resource development and the management of change. He was appointed head of the Manpower Division in 1989, with overall responsibility for such work as demographic change, the development of IT skills, and women in management. He edited *Training and Competitiveness* with Robert Mackay, a review of training policy and its relationship to economic performance, and contributed to papers for the National Economic Development Council. He joined the then Institute of Personnel Management in November 1992. Currently he is responsible to the Professional Policy Committee of the Institute of Personnel and Development (IPD) for the development of policy, research activities, and the forums network. He is also responsible for the library and information service and the legal advisory service. A major review initiated by him of the development of people management and the role of personnel within this has resulted in the consultative document *Managing people – the changing frontiers* (1993) and the position paper *People make the difference* (1994).

Clive Wright's career in the computer industry has spanned over 20 years, during which he worked initially as a software engineer and subsequently in personnel. He has held senior line personnel positions, specialising in compensation over the last 10 years. Currently he is Manager, Corporate Remuneration for compensation and benefits policies and procedures in all ICL companies worldwide. This covers 24,000 employees in over 40 countries, from the person who makes the tea to the chairman and chief executive. He is also responsible for expatriate policy and assignments, and for advising the company on the personnel implications of European Union legislation and programmes.

Acknowledgements

In presenting this publication, the Institute would like to record its appreciation of the research carried out on its behalf by the IPD's Working Party on Pay Drift and Inflation:

Helen Murlis (Chair)	Vice-President – Pay and Employment Conditions 1992–1994 and Senior Director, Hay Management Consultants
Robert Elliott	Professor of Economics, Aberdeen University
David Guest	Professor of Occupational Psychology, Birkbeck College
Peter Ingram	Lecturer in Economics, University of Surrey
Ken Mayhew	Fellow and Tutor in Economics, Pembroke College, Oxford University
John Stevens	Director of Professional Policy, IPD
Andrew Strathdee	EMEA Compensation and Benefits Manager, Lotus Development Corporation
Katharine Turner	Manager – Remuneration and Benefits Policy, BT plc
Malcolm Weaver	Senior Consultant, Hay Management Consultants
Stephen Wood	IPD Research Fellow, London School of Economics
Clive Wright	Manager – Corporate Remuneration, ICL plc

The IPD would also like to record its thanks to the authors who contributed to this project on their behalf, and to Oonagh Ryden who managed the project on behalf of the Institute. Thanks are also due to Stephen Palmer, Michael Armstrong and Josie Pottinger, IPD Vice-President – Pay and Employment Conditions, who provided invaluable guidance during this project.

Finally, and not least, the Institute wishes to express its gratitude to all those individuals in the case-study organisations who participated in the research and gave us the benefit of their thoughts and time, including: Malcolm Rennard of the Employment Service, Terry Moseley of the Civil Aviation Authority (recently retired), Ray McAfee of HM Customs and Excise, Philip Bradney and Clive Bull (formerly) of Derby City General Hospital, Helen Jobson of Mercury Communications Ltd, Fiona Yates of First Direct, Clive Wright of ICL plc, and David Bower and Marcus Sinclair Taylor of Rover Group Ltd.

The views expressed in this report are those of the authors and do not necessarily reflect those of the Institute.

CHAPTER ONE

Pay and the Business Agenda

Stephen Palmer

> The starting-point for taking decisions about pay is not an analysis of the merits of different kinds of grading structure, incremental patterns, data collection techniques and the like. The starting-point is a consideration of what the organisation is, and what it is seeking to do . . . Organisations have an implicit or explicit understanding of their mission. To serve that mission . . . they have a marketing strategy, a financial strategy, a production strategy, a personnel strategy and other strategic plans appropriate to their kind of business . . . Pay is part of the personnel strategy . . . It follows that pay cannot be treated in isolation: that management must co-ordinate decisions about pay with other decisions about personnel, and ensure that personnel decisions are integrated with the overall management of the business.
> *Report by Hay Management Consultants to the Inquiry into Civil Service Pay, 1982*

Wise words in 1982, and wise words now. And yet, how many of us have attended conferences recently on remuneration practices, or read books on the subject, and learned anything about the business environment and its impact on pay policy? Too often we can be left with the feeling that pay practices just emerge from nowhere and for no particular reason. But pay doesn't exist in a vacuum; it should derive from personnel policies which themselves are driven by the business agenda facing the organisation.

In this chapter we will look at the long- and short-term influences on business, the sort of personnel responses they will require, and the role of pay within those responses.

The business agenda

Nobody doubts that organisations in the UK – perhaps for different reasons – face some severe challenges. That is just as true for the public sector as it is for the private – although the challenges may be different for the two sectors.

As a nation we have some longer-term problems to address.

World trade has been growing consistently faster than world economic growth since the mid-1950s. As a major trading nation Britain has benefited from the increased size of the 'cake', and our share of world trade has been fairly consistent over the last decade or so. But our position is already under threat; for example, our performance measured against just one of our major competitors, Japan, shows that the UK's per capita export growth has risen by less than half that of the Japanese since 1945. And if we have not performed that well on the export front, it has also been bad news for our import performance, where the penetration of manufactured goods doubled from 18.4 per cent to 35.7 per cent between 1975 and 1992. Our proclivity to import led to severe trade imbalances in the past and the subsequent weakness of sterling which, in turn, fed through into higher inflation.

Meanwhile, all established economies face growing competition as the structure of world trade changes. Real pressures on markets already come from the Asian 'tigers' such as South Korea, Taiwan, Singapore, and Hong Kong (see Figure 1). Added to these will be the rapidly industrialising

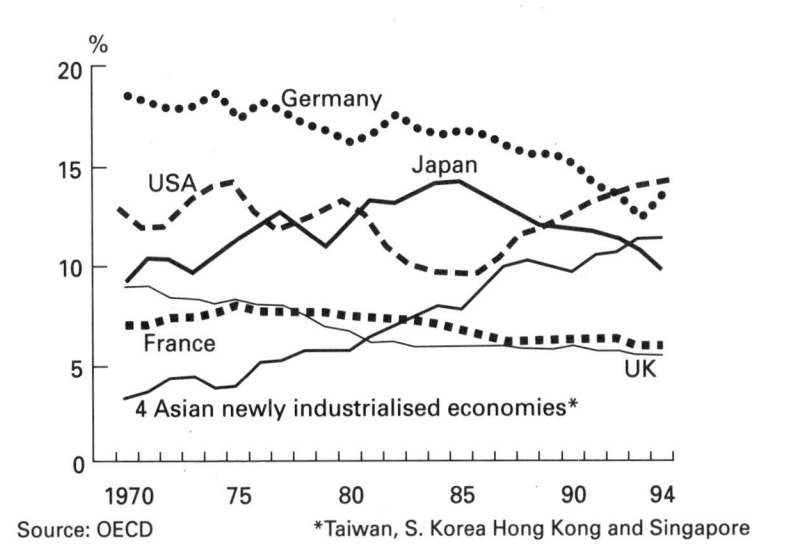

Figure 1 *Share of world manufacturing exports*

[Chart showing share of world manufacturing exports from 1970 to 1994 for Germany, Japan, USA, France, UK, and 4 Asian newly industrialised economies. Source: OECD. *Taiwan, S. Korea Hong Kong and Singapore]

China, India, Thailand and Malaysia; and although they may not pose any immediate threat, few doubt that the Eastern European countries, with their access to cheap raw materials and labour, will be formidable players in years to come.

These pressures are compounded by the ease with which capital and technical know-how can be transferred around the world. Hitherto essential stages in the economic development of whole economies can now be bypassed, so speeding up the process of development and 'catching up'. Recent examples include the rise of Spain to number among the leading car manufacturers of Europe, and the rapid investment of western economies, and others, in Eastern Europe. The movement of capital and know-how reduces the reliance of developing countries on one product, and increases their scope to compete in traditional western product markets.

It so happens that Britain too has gained from direct

foreign investment. That has a lot to do with lower employment costs compared to other developed countries, largely because of lower social charges than lower pay rates *per se* (see Figure 2). But British companies and their employees also face the prospect of increasing competition from a growing number of countries where employment costs and government charges are even lower. Indeed, it could be argued that the unskilled manual worker in manufacturing truly does face an international labour market!

Figure 2 *Comparative international labour costs 1994*

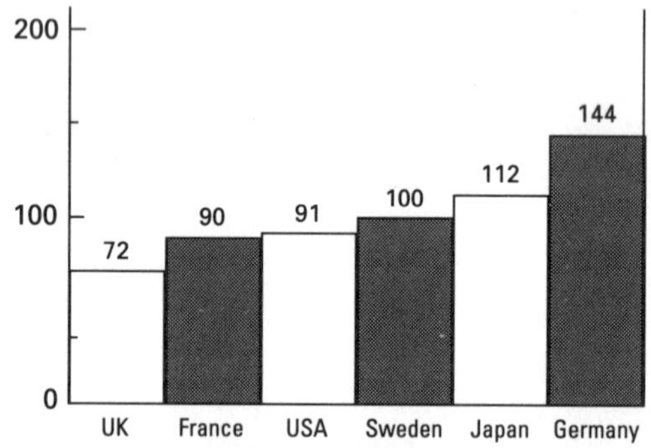

UK	France	USA	Sweden	Japan	Germany
72	90	91	100	112	144

Source: SAF

Developing technologies mean substantial changes both to business operations and to the structure of markets and economies. The globalisation of markets occasioned by increasing information flows clearly has implications for marketing, branding and the size of organisations. The pace of technological change and innovation erodes the traditional lead-in time advantages enjoyed by the developed economies. The movement of capital and know-how aids the transfer of technology to underdeveloped regions. At the same time, the rapidity of innovation raises the rate of obsolescence, allowing few companies the luxury of sitting back while the rest catch up. Consequently, minimising the innovation and process times of getting new products to market becomes crucial to future success.

Of course, increased globalisation allows organisations to shop around for the best service from suppliers – and not just in manufacturing; service sector companies face the same pressure. Buyers can impose standards that are not just 'the best in the area' or even 'the best in the country', but 'the best in the world'. The result is that suppliers face increasingly exacting specifications and cost constraints, so that organisations that may not otherwise consider themselves competing in world markets suddenly find themselves vicariously subject to the challenges of global competition.

So employers want to create an enterprise culture where employees are expected, and empowered, to contribute to business success through using their own initiative to solve problems within a much more fluid and less prescriptive managerial structure. In a highly competitive world, people really are an organisation's most important asset.

Finally, organisations increasingly realise that they cannot expect to operate immune from the requirements of the community which permits their operation. Becoming involved in the community means not just a commitment to reducing pollution or improving the environment, but also investment for the 'public good' in the community itself. Both approaches imply a greater acceptance on the part of employers that their economic power and their freedom to operate are ultimately limited by society at large.

A major part of the response of organisations to all these challenges has been to place the emphasis on their employees, particularly increasing value for money. Here, the UK faces other, shorter-term, problems. For a start, economic growth has faltered (see Figure 3). It slowed in 1995, and forecasts for 1996 point to a further decline in the rate of increase. Even the Chancellor appeared to have shaded down forecasts for 1996 within two weeks of making his budget speech. And because growth has slowed, so has the rate of decline in unemployment – helped by the increasing number of people entering the labour market.

Figure 3 *UK economic growth*
(annual % change)

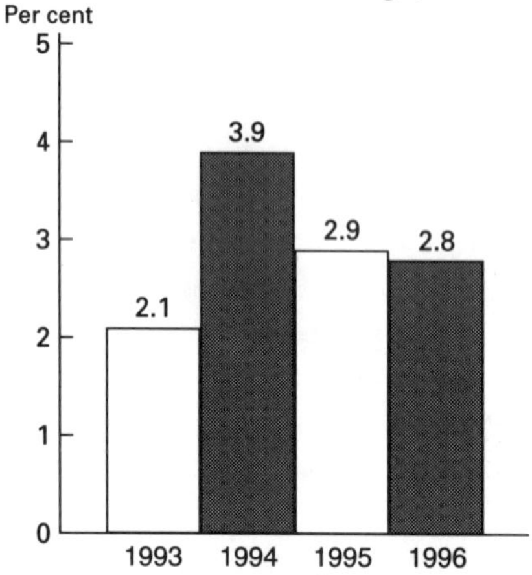

```
Per cent
5
4        3.9
3              2.9   2.8
    2.1
2
1
0
   1993  1994  1995  1996
```

Source: CBI/OECD

Inflation moved up in 1995 but peaked around Christmas. Forecasts now suggest inflationary pressures will be low in 1996, perhaps around 2.5 per cent. This is certainly low by the UK's historic standards, but it is still some way ahead of major competitors. This relatively high inflation is part of the price we pay for devaluing our currency.

Our productivity performance in manufacturing has fallen back, but earnings growth has remained practically static. The result is that UK unit labour costs have started to rise again, just as our major competitors are achieving falls (see Figure 4). Let's not fool ourselves: UK earnings growth may be close to an historic low by our standards, but it's high compared to key competitors'.

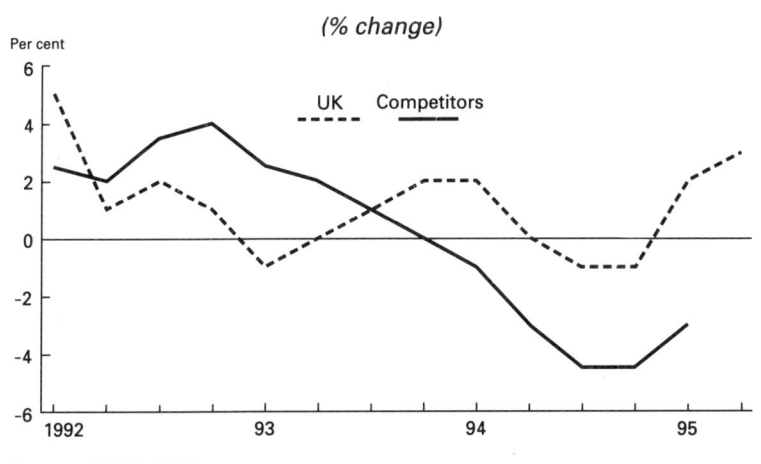

Figure 4 *Unit labour cost trends*
(% change)

Source: OECD, IMF

Were the current relative earnings and productivity performance to carry on, UK industry would lose the benefits of the post-ERM devaluation in just five years.

In trying to tackle these difficulties it is as well to bear in mind there are other problems. Fixed investment per head in the UK is some way behind competitors. And this is reflected in productivity per head which in the UK is just over half that of the USA, and 10 to 15 per cent behind Germany and Japan (see Figure 5).

That is why the response from UK organisations must put the emphasis on improving the performance – in whatever form that takes – of their employees.

Parallel pressures in the public sector

The pressures for change in the public sector stem also from increased competition, although from a somewhat different source. As Chapter 5 highlights, Government macro-economic policy is the biggest pressure because,

Figure 5 *International manufacturing productivity*

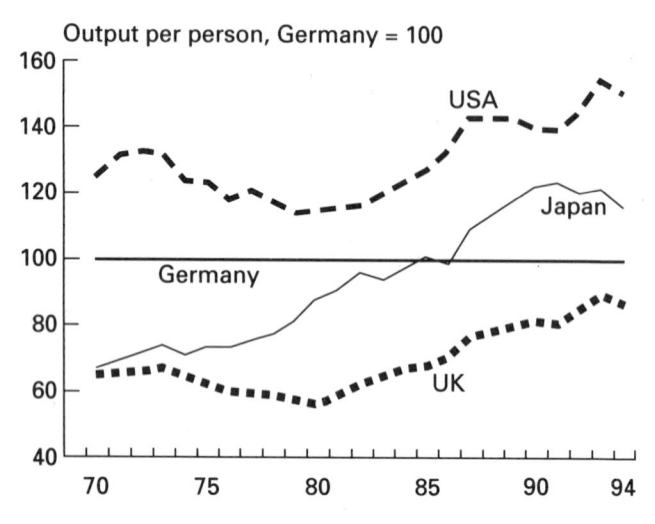

Output per person, Germany = 100

Source: Bart van Ark, University of Groningen,
Updated by CBI estimates for 1991-1994

with its focus on cutting costs and increasing efficiency, it emphasises the need to contain public expenditure.

The response from public sector organisations has taken a number of forms not very different from those of the private sector. Pay systems are being designed which are 'fit for purpose' and do not assume that every public sector employer or employee group is the same as any other; perhaps the only exception is individualised performance-related pay which the Government has appeared to see as a panacea for all pay ills. Like their private sector counterparts, public sector bodies have brought in, or are bringing in, competency-based approaches to managing and improving performance. More fundamental has been the drive to decentralise pay bargaining; although still comparatively rare in local government, this approach is now the rule in the civil service and is spreading through the NHS.

It is not difficult, from the case-studies, to see why. For the Employment Service the existing Civil Service arrangements were too coarse and caused real headaches because they did not differentiate between the demands of different jobs and their location. The result was that some perceived 'softer' jobs in the policy areas would be very attractive compared with more challenging frontline management pools in posts at the same grade delivering the service in deprived inner city areas, for example. The Service sought to overhaul its existing performance appraisal system and implement competency-based vacancy filling and use pay in an integrated way to support these.

The Civil Aviation Authority (CAA) also found that the centrally determined Civil Service terms and conditions under which they operated got in the way of attempts to change organisational structures and working practices. Managers themselves were saying that the pay system was too complex and difficult to understand (there were, for example, over 100 allowances introduced at various times to buy flexibility), with no clear link between pay and performance, and no discernable effect on motivation. The CAA's response has been to put pay structures fully under managerial control.

The public sector has other issues to deal with, not found in the private sector: the five pay review bodies have a large say over the rates of pay of 1.5 million people; the difficulty of measuring the output of groups such as nurses or teachers can limit the effectiveness and acceptance of performance-related pay schemes; and the up-front investment needed to introduce change is often either missing or very limited, a point made by the Employment Service. The funding of agencies and departments does not allow a direct link between the funding for pay awards and the performance of the organisation. While the response to increased competition and reduced resources may be similar to those of private sector organisations, the circumstances in which public sector bodies must manage those responses most certainly is not.

Experiences of the case-studies

The organisations in our eight case-studies have had to react to many of the pressures outlined above. In the early 1980s ICL had to face a strengthening pound which, coupled with a price war in the computer market, put severe pressure on margins. Later, tougher Government tendering requirements and a big growth in the PC market reduced traditional sources of income. All these together resulted in over a decade of having to focus on productivity and the need to be commercially competitive; a saga that is by no means over, or is ever likely to be. Mercury is another high-tech company, and one which grew very rapidly in the 1980s, but it, too, had to retrench in the face of increasing competition from cable companies and price retaliation from BT. Rover, in the guise of British Leyland, had to contend with appalling industrial relations, inflexible working practices and a poor quality image, while all the time facing growing competition from the Far East, especially Japan.

First Direct was slightly different. Here the organisation came into being as a response to evidence of growing public dissatisfaction with traditional banking services and to changing customer banking habits which placed less emphasis on the High Street branch to deliver services.

In the public sector, all of our case-studies found themselves masters of their own destinies as the Government devolved responsibilities to them. To a greater or lesser extent all found that traditional, centrally determined, terms and conditions were no longer appropriate to meet the cost and competitive challenges they faced. Derby City

General Hospital Trust was under pressure to deliver greater volumes of healthcare at higher quality but at a lower cost. Like all health service providers it found almost unlimited demand but distinctly limited funding. HM Customs & Excise perhaps faced some unique pressures, for in addition to the external pressures from Government to cut costs, deregulation and the requirements of the Citizens Charter, they needed to react to the implications of the single European market, the growing sophistication of those intent on evading duty, and the VAT implications of the growing complexity of business itself.

It is worth noting, however, that the response of all of these organisations was first to establish an overall strategy for dealing with their own business challenges, part of which included a human resource strategy, and within which was included a new remuneration approach. Pay was important, but only to the extent that it helped deliver business objectives. At ICL a fundamental review of company strategy drove the development of a new personnel strategy. It was because First Direct was primarily customer-driven as a business objective, that the human resource policy has been to develop a skills-based complement to achieve it. The CAA found that it had to relate compensation to the needs of the business, particularly to deal with severe recruitment and retention problems which could not be handled via the existing centrally negotiated national pay agreements for the Civil Service. And the Employment Service set out to prepare a specific pay and grading structure which delivered value for money and supported the delivery of its own business targets.

Employees and the business agenda

As the First Direct case-study concludes, 'They realise that, in order to keep ahead of their competition, they will need to continue to harness the enthusiasm and potential of individuals within their business.'

So, what are employers going to look for from their employees?

Certainly, in the early 1980s, and again more recently, employers sought to raise output per employee through a process of demanning along with the introduction of approaches such as multiskilling, contracting out, numerical flexibility and teamworking. These changes have taken place at all levels in the organisation. More productivity improvements will be required in the future. Greater efficiency has already been achieved through cutting waste and this is a continuing process; it is also an area where a major contribution has come from employees who are able to carry out, for example, basic maintenance, match their working hours to business needs, or do a variety of different jobs. Again, further improvements will be required.

Total quality concepts have played an important part in employers' drive for quality improvements, an issue raised by all of our case-studies. In the past, the responsibility for quality may have been hived into separate control groups. Now, the emphasis has to be on quality as a concern of all employees and a part of everyone's job. In a similar way, there has also been an increasing emphasis on the customer in order to establish competitive advantage, and that, too, needs employee commitment.

In many markets future competitive success depends on how well an organisation can harness the intellectual strength of its employees to research and develop new products and services. By extension, organisations will need continuous improvements in the way they operate. That means harnessing every employee's ideas for improvements in the way he or she works.

These approaches remain essential for the rest of the decade and beyond. They pose a fundamental challenge to the traditional wage/labour 'contract'. In its place open-ended contracts have already started to emerge, providing for unique employer/employee relationships that can develop over time. Achieving these objectives, within a looser employer/employee relationship, while retaining the commitment of employees will be a major objective. We consider some of the issues in Chapter 3. It also seems clear that getting employees 'on board' is likely to be more successful if unjustifiable differences in treatment are eradicated. If they want their employees to drop demarcation boundaries, employers will probably need to drop theirs as well. Both ICL and Rover have introduced single-status arrangements and set considerable store by a well developed sense of mutual responsibility within the 'psychological contract' implied in employer/employee relationships.

The personnel response

For the majority of organisations future competitive success points to a significant change in employment policies. The major changes are already evident:

- greater emphasis on the training and development of employees including, increasingly, employees in 'peripheral' groups
- development of flatter and more flexible organisational structures with greater delegation of responsibility and authority
- management styles which take account of the demands of a better educated and more self-confident workforce
- increased attention to the need for fast, frequent and efficient communication between different levels of employee
- greater emphasis on individuals as team members, extending their responsibilities and building their commitment to the values and goals of the organisation

- implementation of reward strategies focused on performance and taking account of the expectations of individual employees.

Where does pay fit into all this?

Pay – a place in the sun?

The way in which thinking on pay has changed, from the administered and inflexible strait-jacket of the 1970s to the agent of change in the 1990s, is covered in Chapter 2. The case-studies later on in the book give examples of the scope and role of pay in leading organisations faced with competitive challenges. But five important trends (sometimes termed 'new pay') seem to be emerging: variable pay, broad-banding, competency-related pay, flexible benefits and employee communications. These deserve close attention.

Variable pay
Variable pay is 'at risk' pay linked to individual, team and/or corporate performance. It specifically is not base pay (including consolidated merit awards), overtime or shift pay, or benefits. Variable payment systems cover approaches such as bonuses and incentive schemes, profit sharing, share schemes or 'one-off' performance awards. The fundamental features are that the payments are re-earnable and not consolidated into basic pay, although cash payments made under such schemes may be taken into account in determining pensions or other benefit entitlements. This means that payments can go down, as well as up, in line with performance.

Survey evidence shows a growing interest in variable payments systems in the UK. There are a number of reasons for this.

Firstly, there is the influence of American experience.

In the USA there exists a widespread and growing use of variable pay systems – particularly gainsharing plans – across the economy. There has been a tendency for American compensation approaches to emerge in the UK in recent years and variable pay is unlikely to be any different.

Secondly, although employers are not abandoning individualised performance-related pay – indeed, two-thirds of UK employers now claim to have performance-related pay for some or all of their employees – there are some signs that these schemes may have gone as far as they can in improving motivation. Research from the then Institute of Manpower Studies in the early 1990s (now the Institute of Employment Studies) into the attitudes of 1,000 employees covered by performance-related pay showed that they, at least, did not believe that the awards had made any impact on their motivation. This is a point to which we return in Chapter 3. In the early 1980s, individualised performance-related pay was a key part of private sector remuneration strategy underpinning changes to company culture to produce a sharper performance focus. In the 1990s, the focus is moving away from a simplistic reliance on performance-related pay to an equal emphasis on building and rewarding skills and capabilities.

The problem for employers is that while the pay outcome of employee appraisals might be variable as between different individuals, the actual payment itself is not variable. That is because, under most systems, performance awards are consolidated into basic pay – in other words the employees' annual movement through their grade and related pay band is related to performance. In the eyes of some employers, this has led to nothing more than a souped-up, and expensive, version of annual increments if only because the reality is that most 'fully satisfactory' employees fare about the same in terms of pay increases as they would have done with fixed, service-related increments. So, whatever the advantages of performance-related pay, (and few people argue with the principle, whatever they think of the process), it can still ratchet up fixed costs. In this regard it is interesting that HM Customs only consolidates performance awards up to a certain point; above this they are paid as non-consolidated and non-pensionable bonuses. At First Direct base pay reflects the market rates for skills; productivity is recognised by bonuses.

By going down, as well as up, in line with performance, variable pay allows costs to be more closely aligned with what the organisation can afford. That, incidentally, reduces the pressure on employers to cut manning during temporary downturns in the economy. These ideas have had more success in the pay and benefits environment in the USA; in the UK they are more common at executive levels than lower down – there is a limit to the amount of variability employees on relatively low earnings are able to take.

Thirdly, many organisations now want to encourage a culture of teamworking instead of (or as well as) one of pure individualism. There has, for example, been a steady move to functional flexibility, that is, training a multiskilled workforce to be capable of performing a range of tasks – including basic and preventive maintenance, without the traditional craft demarcations that used to be such a disruptive and expensive feature of British industry in the past.

This trend has been coupled with significant delayering and the devolution of responsibility and authority ever closer to the production unit. With the emphasis on Japanese-style, quality-driven production methods, employees at all levels have to have more power over working methods. Such 'empowerment' sits easier with pay structures which encourage a teamworking approach than perhaps it does with individualised performance-related pay alone, unless effective teamwork is rewarded within that framework – an increasingly common phenomenon.

Finally, the fourth reason for the growing interest in some sorts of variable pay is the operation of the tax system. Tax relief of certain types of share plans and on Inland Revenue approved profit-related pay schemes has raised the profile of these approaches for employers and employees alike. Whether reward strategies driven purely by tax arrangements will ever put down deep roots in the nation's remuneration psyche remains to be seen; share plans do appear to be increasingly attractive, but generally for reasons other than pay (eg employee involvement), particularly at lower-grade levels. The principal gain so far experienced from well-implemented profit-related pay schemes is greater financial understanding within the workforce.

Broadbanding
The drive to greater pay flexibility has aroused interest in broadbanding approaches – that is, where pay ranges are wider, and grades are fewer. A recent CBI/Hay survey[1] found that more than one in four of the organisations covered already had fewer than 10 grades, although the average was still 16 or more.

Why are companies introducing broadbanding? Nearly two-thirds of organisations said it would provide for more pay flexibility. It fits better with flatter organisations, where upwards promotion through grades becomes rarer. And it reduces the unhealthy emphasis on grade status which can stand in the way of building project teams and individual experience across different areas of an organisation.

But it does put an emphasis on developing employees as a quid pro quo for the fewer promotion opportunities now open to them. The Rover case-study notes that delayering results in a reduction in promotions and grade changes; the firm has found that making other and wider personal development opportunities available has contributed to sustaining employees' motivation.

Competency-related pay
Other salary systems growing in importance are those related to the acquisition and use of competencies or which link pay in part to the acquisition and use of defined and often accredited skills. This ties some element of pay to an employee's inputs to the job and not just to outputs. By focusing not just on 'what you do' but 'how you do it', competency-related pay can encourage the sorts of behaviours – communication skills, customer care, team contribution – that organisations want to encourage. The same CBI/Hay survey found that 18 per cent of organisations already use skills- or competency-related pay today, and a further 25 per cent plan to move down this route over the next two years. Organisations give a number of reasons for doing so: to improve and support training and development, and to provide a better and more holistic basis for managing performance, being particularly important.

We have noted above that ICL is giving the same status to the development of skills and capabilities in its remuneration policies as is currently enjoyed by performance-related pay alone. First Direct has introduced a skills-based structure with three objectives: as a means of managing performance because employees now have a clear idea of what is required in terms of skills and performance; as a means of reward – base pay is derived from the skills required and the appropriate market rates (and movements in rates); and to encourage employees to pursue their own career development.

Derby City General Hospital Trust has developed a competency model which is used to define individual roles and the typical characteristics of high performers. The new pay structure is flatter with longer grade ranges.

Flexible benefits
Cash pay might account for the bulk of employment costs,

but benefits packages can cost between 10 and 14 per cent for the average employee, (and over 100 per cent for senior managers if share options are included). Yet at present it is not at all clear that employers think they are getting value for the money they spend. A CBI/Towers Perrin survey[2] in 1992 found that a third of employers did not think their employees understood benefit content; around half felt there was a clear need to improve employee appreciation of benefits; and 84 per cent considered that employee awareness of benefit cost was 'poor'.

In the same survey, employers noted major changes in the shape of their workforces over the previous five years, with more people from dual income families, more females, and an ageing workforce. Yet in all these cases changes to benefit provision in recognition of a changing workforce was much lower. Hardly surprising, perhaps, that employees are less enthusiastic about their benefits package than employers think they should be.

Hardly surprising, also, that employers are reassessing benefits packages both to reduce costs and align them more closely with the needs of their employees. Their response suggests moves to implementing total remuneration rather than pay-plus-benefits; to matching benefit philosophy to general corporate objectives and business plans; and to providing flexibility in choice of benefits. Even so, any move to flexible benefits is likely to be evolutionary rather than revolutionary: only 5 per cent of the respondents to the CBI/Hay survey operate flexible benefit arrangements now, although a further 25 per cent are considering flexibility as an option.

Mercury has already gone down this route and introduced individual choice into benefit package design both to make employees aware of benefit cost (around £50 million a year) and to recognise employees' differing needs and requirements.

ICL on the other hand, once it found that a substantial

proportion of the workforce felt the benefit package could be better communicated, introduced an annual personalised statement for employees outlining all the benefits they received.

Communications and involvement
It is clear that pay has an important part to play in changing attitudes and behaviours. Organisations trying to bring about change have learned that it helps to have employees on-side; what many also seem to feel is that this doesn't just mean getting union agreement, but the agreement and commitment of individual employees themselves. That means moving away from the traditional approach by which the union(s) are the only communication channel – an approach, incidentally, which often meant the shop floor having information before their supervisors – to a more sophisticated system of direct communication with employees.

Well, that's the theory anyway, and no one can doubt the effort that employers have put in to improving communications with all of their employees. Unfortunately, a distinct feeling exists, even among employers, that the more popular communication media are not achieving their communication objectives. For example, the CBI/Towers Perrin survey in 1992 asked employers to list the communication methods they used, and rate them for effectiveness. The authors of the report note with disarming understatement that 'the survey highlighted an interesting discrepancy between the most commonly used channels of communication and the most effective ones'.

The written word – memos, newsletters, booklets – predominated, despite the fact that these approaches attracted some of the lowest scores for effectiveness (see Figure 6). On the other hand, face-to-face communication methods scored very highly for effectiveness, but tended to be comparatively less widespread. There is probably no single answer; the Employment Service used a variety of media

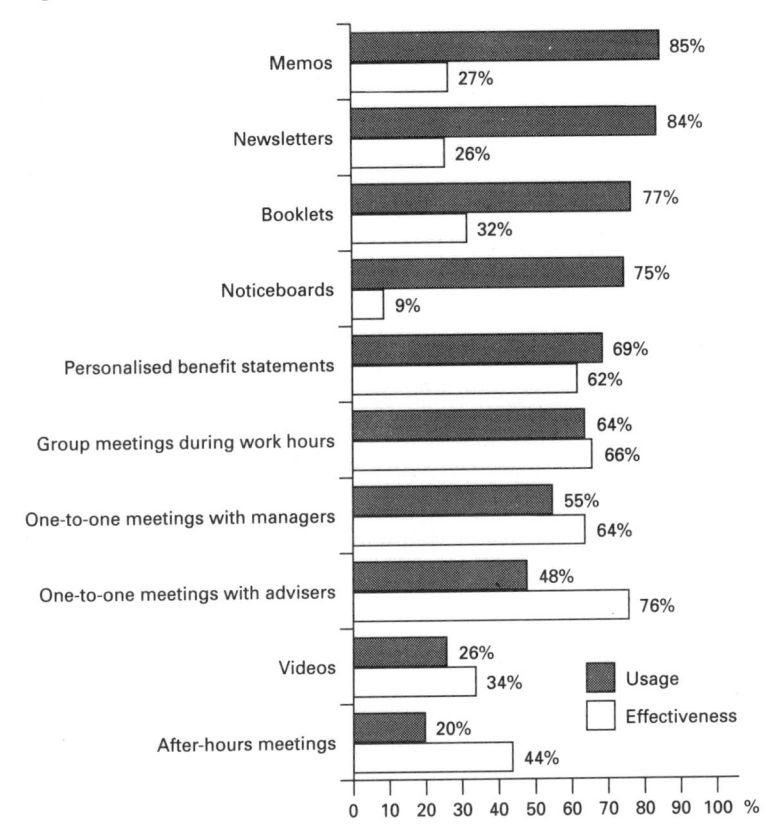

Figure 6 *Communication channels: usage and effectiveness*

Channel	Usage	Effectiveness
Memos	85%	27%
Newsletters	84%	26%
Booklets	77%	32%
Noticeboards	75%	9%
Personalised benefit statements	69%	62%
Group meetings during work hours	64%	66%
One-to-one meetings with managers	55%	64%
One-to-one meetings with advisers	48%	76%
Videos	26%	34%
After-hours meetings	20%	44%

Source: CBI/Towers Perrin

to communicate plans, work in progress and decisions on pay and grading changes. Their own analysis suggested that no one medium will get the message over to the entire workforce and as a consequence success has been patchy.

Communication isn't a one-way street. Many of the organisations had taken care to learn and track employee attitudes as the new strategies were implemented. ICL carries out annual employee attitude surveys and only linked appraisals to pay once it was clear that employees found the appraisal system itself fair. As we note above, the driving force for greater effort to communicate the benefits package followed on a special employee survey which showed that 40 per cent of employees felt it needed improving. In 1992 the company published a comprehensive employee booklet covering job evaluation, salary scales, grades, appraisal and major benefits, the first of its kind in the company.

Clearly, bringing about change will be easier and more effective if employees know why and what you are trying to do, so don't overlook how you communicate with them. Nor, the evidence of the case-studies suggests, should organisations ignore the knowledge and talent that employees have, and which can be tapped to determine remuneration structures. The Derby City General Hospital Trust explains that the heavy involvement of staff in designing a competency-related pay system was 'a key element of success'. A fifth of nurses and midwives took part as members of focus groups to identify the distinctive contributions of their professions and to fill out an extensive questionnaire about the key roles and the key qualities of good performers. First Direct set out to ensure not only that its HR strategy complemented the business objectives but also to involve employees in its development by identifying the core skills and producing role profiles.

Involvement can pay off in other ways too. During the last eight years of its operation, Rover's employee suggestion scheme delivered audited annual savings of £8.5 million, and played a major part in encouraging employee contribution during those years.

Conclusion

The remaining chapters of this book examine pay from a variety of angles and in a variety of circumstances. If there was only one theme to emerge (in fact there are many) it would be that pay is only part of the business of making organisations competitive. But it is an important part and, unlike the pay administrators of the past, today's compensation experts have the tools and the authority to design pay systems which will deliver not just crude improvements in output, but changes in employee behaviours, improved organisational cultures and an employee focus on issues such as customer satisfaction, quality and efficiency.

As we note in the final chapter, not all senior management will understand the active role that pay can take in bringing about the competitive organisations they want. The first task of the compensation specialist may be educating the bosses. This book should help you to do that.

CHAPTER TWO

Pay at the Crossroads

John Stevens

In the opening chapter we looked at the business agenda – in both the public and private sectors – the HR response, and the role of pay within that response. In this chapter we look in more depth at some of the practical and philosophical issues.

Two debates on pay exist alongside, but without touching, each other. The first is a highly visible discussion about the relationship between pay and inflation. This is the traditional 'political' debate. It sees people in their negotiating role, trying to keep ahead of inflation or seeking pay increases irrespective of their economic justification. The second debate has to do with the role of pay in the management of people. This debate, if it surfaces at all in the media, does so mainly in the context of exceptionally high industrial tribunal awards in equal opportunities cases or the pay and benefits packages of senior managers or the 'failures' of performance-related pay. The two debates run like railway lines towards the horizon, linked yet not touching. Bringing these debates into contact with each other or, for that matter, altering the form so that they take on a 'real world' dimension requires human resource practitioners to highlight and deal with a considerable amount of historical baggage. The challenges are considered.

The need for pay literacy

'Strategic pay', as opposed to 'administered pay', requires a high degree of literacy from those who operate pay systems. Even personnel professionals who have specialised in compensation and benefits practice over many years are having to adjust. Knowing how pay can be used to affect behaviour is becoming more important while the ritual dance of collective negotiation becomes less important. But the requirement to understand what is going on, and why, is now stronger.

We have seen that organisations under intense competitive pressures need to review objectives and the contribution expected from their people. In particular, line managers and chief executives must have a sophisticated understanding of people management issues more generally. This includes the adjustment of employee attitudes: accepting (and communicating) that 'feel good' is about the size of *real* increases and not inflated *money* increases. A pay increase of 7.5 per cent recognising excellent performance with the cost of living at 3.5 per cent still feels less than an increase of 14 per cent with the cost of living up by 14 per cent.

The challenge of low inflation

Over a long period, almost every group in society – Government, employers, trade unions and those on fixed incomes – has agreed that it would be 'a good thing' if inflation could be kept low and we could move away from the pervasive inflationary psychology of the last 30 years. But it has proved remarkably difficult to align longer-term objectives and short-term interests. An 'if this is a free for all, we're part of the all' philosophy is all too understandable. Many people, notably those who became house owners when inflation was rising, benefited substantially in real terms from the effects of inflation on debt and property values.

For organisations, too, inflation has been both a good and an evil. It has introduced uncertainty into pricing and caused difficulties in export markets; but it has also lowered the real cost of debt. Meanwhile, pay has not really proved difficult in the past to manage in a period of inflation. Indeed, the importance of having a satisfied workforce keeping up with, or 'slightly ahead of', the going rate has proved an easier master to serve than the more general 'national interest' of containing inflation.

Rising inflation is a receding threat and managing wage drift looks likely to be of academic interest for some time to come. Of course, the return of the sort of inflationary behaviour 'normal' in the UK is still eagerly awaited by economic commentators. Regular warnings of the evils of returning inflation continue to appear in the newspapers. Although pay increases have crept up slightly in the last year, they have now (in early 1996) plateaued and a feeling prevails that pay and price increases will stay at relatively low levels for some time to come. We also shouldn't forget that even in the tight labour market of the late 1980s inflationary wage pressures were lower than might have been expected from previous experience, and wages grew less during the trough of the 1990–92 recession than they did in the same period in the previous cycle, suggesting that a new realism about pay was already having an influence on expectations.

High levels of pay: an old debate – a recent phenomenon

Large (and annual) pay increases are a relatively new phenomenon; they did not exist until fairly recently. Inflation has been a matter of concern in the last 30 years, particularly as it has been consistently higher in the UK than in major competitor countries. But it was not until 1973 that pay increases soared to levels which were out of all proportion to underlying productivity increases. In the political climate of the mid-1970s inflation seemed more important than the level of productivity or profitability as a determinant of real improvements in living standards and, particularly, wealth. So why should more realism in pay determination *now* be more likely to hold back the pressures for pay inflation?

Strangely, the pay debate in the 1970s paid little attention to the link between inflation and wealth. Partly, of course, this reflected the fact that at the time the growth in home ownership was only just getting under way. Many of those covered by collective bargaining were still in public rented accommodation. But the pay debate equally had little connection with the ability of employers to pay. The language of debate embraced an annual round, the cost of living (which provided a minimum target) and comparability between groups. All too often it ignored profitability, achievement of organisational strategies and a place in the economy of the future.

The annual pay round and comparability

Government pay policies matched and reinforced the rhetoric of the day: increases had to be at least twelve months apart, thus introducing or confirming the concept of the annual round; increases took into account price increases and sought to guarantee real pay advances; they even sought to link pay and non-pay state benefits (including rent controls and tax policy in the 'social contracts' much talked about in the mid-1970s); they also acknowledged the power of comparability by limiting pay increases to a general national formula, by setting up public sector pay review bodies, or operating through wage councils and the fair wages resolution to ensure 'a decency threshold of pay'.

In the 1980s and 1990s most of these statutory mechanisms were dismantled in favour of market mechanisms. The 'ability to pay' argument has become dominant. But beneath the surface, the annual round, the cost of living, and comparability live on in the collective consciousness, rising to the surface now and again for a breath of air. Even today, only if organisations are in serious trouble do employees accept the need for a pay freeze or cut in purchasing power. Pay restraint in the public sector has been used successfully in the last few years as one means of containing the rise in annual earnings across the economy, but here the evidence is of eventual, and large, 'catching-up' awards even though pay decentralisation is likely to limit the power and speed of such measures.

Continued reference to the retail price index by both employers and employees demonstrates a continuing concern about the real value of pay increases. For most organisations, in periods of growth and recession alike, pay increases in excess of retail price index movements were until recently taken as 'given'. To some extent the relationship persists, but the changes both in perceptions and reality mean that it is now more and more accepted that income improvements do have to be earned by productivity growth, either by changes in work methods or by tighter resourcing. We return to this theme in the final chapter.

The issue of low pay

If there is an emerging exception to this general trend, it lies among low-paid workers. Pay increased less quickly for workers in lower-paid jobs than others after 1980, reversing the effect of flat rate incomes policies during the 1970s. As a result, the gap between the earnings of those at the top of the earnings distribution and those at the bottom became substantially wider after more than 100 years of near-stability. The abolition of wage councils, the growth of part-time working, and the outsourcing of blue collar public sector services have all contributed to this widening of relativities. The reasons for wider dispersion seem to reflect divergent philosophies in the employment of people. One is the importance of developing people – creating an internal labour market and maintaining the real value of rewards. The other is the availability of people with lower-level skills, taking advantage of the outside labour market, and lower rates of pay. The approaches are not mutually exclusive and can be found working in the same organisation; they account for the moral (as opposed to economic) stance of the supporters of a national minimum wage.

The current place of comparability

Developments in the influence of the comparability concept are more difficult to track, but the concept appears to have moved from being dominant, and to some degree sacrosanct, to a less prominent place. When inflation is low there is a much greater spread in the value of pay increases. CBI figures show that during the 1980s more than 50 per cent of manufacturers and 60 per cent of service firms quoted some form of comparability as a strong upward pressure on pay. By August 1993 these figures had fallen to 25 per cent for manufacturing and 40 per cent for services, accompanied by a greater emphasis on the local, rather than the national, pay scene, particularly for employees recruited solely in local labour markets.

How far this is due to the decline in the level of

increases and how far it relates to a longer-term decoupling of pay linkages is difficult to say. Certainly the idea that a pace-setting pay increase by an organisation in the same sector requires a matching award seems now to be largely defunct. However, this perception may turn out to be remarkably shortlived if market pressures mean that increases start to rise again.

Recovery but a lack of optimism

Much is now made of a new concept: the 'feel good' factor. As ideas go, this one is powerful. Why is the Government's opinion poll rating low? The feel good factor is missing. Why are consumers not spending? The feel good factor is missing. Rationally, we all know that it would be best to keep inflationary earnings increases and interest rates below those of competitors, while pursuing a sustainable growth level. But equally, people feel that having survived a major recession they deserve some reward. They point to productivity growth from improvements to quality, cuts in costs, greater flexibility, extended skills, better performance management and appraisal; to emerging skill shortages; and to higher profitability. Employees want a piece of the action and in some way hanker for the large increases which, by sleight of hand, gave big, real and immediate improvements in the past even if they were quickly eroded by inflation. Those who have sharpened their performance in tough conditions have yet to adjust to the size of cash reward currently paid. Some are demotivated by the 'shortfall' in their economic contracts causing a distinct lack of feeling good, and are not 'participating' in the economy, in terms of spending, as they did ten years ago.

Decentralised bargaining: more responsive or less controllable?

More than a decade of decentralisation, divestment, privatisation, market testing and similar developments has led to pay decisions being made at many more points in the economy. In the public sector, decentralisation has presented some organisations, which had previously followed central agreements, with the need to design their own pay systems from scratch. But more generally, employers who have followed national rates seem to be taking the opportunity to act independently. For some this helps to adjust pay to local labour markets; for others it reflects a desire for pay systems that are specific to the organisation.

At least 16 national bargaining agreements, covering well over a million employees, were terminated in the late 1980s – including those of the London clearing banks, the multiple food retailers and the engineering employers. The Civil Service had devolved pay to individual agencies and departments for all staff below senior management level by April 1996 and even the NHS is moving to an extent down a decentralisation road. In the future, flexible employment practices – temporary, contract and 'portfolio working' – will become even more widespread. Pay in the traditional sense will become a less important element of employment costs, and controls will be exercised on an even more decentralised basis. Far from having 'co-ordinated collective bargaining' as was suggested by some unions in the late 1980s (and by some employers in the late 1970s), to bring about the sorts of low inflation benefits enjoyed by the likes of Sweden, Australia, Germany and Japan, we now have the precise opposite. No one yet knows what this decentralised model will deliver in the long term. Will market and cost pressures help to control pay at sensible levels, or will leap-frogging and even 'pattern bargaining' fuel a pay spiral? We don't know. Much depends on employee perceptions of total rewards, the loyalties they have to 'good employers' and the costing balance of the economic and psychological contract. In that regard, personnel management will be a critical factor. If there is a resurgence of employee power, albeit on a new model, there is no doubt that unions will seek to manage decentralisation for the benefit of their members. Their response is, however, likely to be both more sophisticated and more complex than the straight 'parity' issues of 20 years ago.

Moving to a new pay realism

While the dangers of a pay explosion are held at bay by market pressures on prices, and public finances place similar pressures on organisations in the public sector, there is also another reason for why a new realism in pay is emerging. Pay is switching from a negotiating or 'pay and rations' issue and is becoming part of a web of practices aimed at developing organisational outcomes by changing attitudes and actions. Pay is no longer treated simply as a motivator to achieve higher levels of effort. It is used to reward the acquisition of skills, the achievement of objectives, the development of careers and the adoption of particular types of behaviour.

Flatter organisational structures and more candidates for promotion than can possibly be accommodated have led to a thorough-going reappraisal of the place of pay in the way in which organisations and people are managed. Organisations have been delayering, making significant changes in structure and responsibilities held at different levels with the objective of increasing customer orientation, reducing inertia and increasing responsiveness, and developing commitment and initiative. Decisions in such organisations can be made more quickly. Providing a reward strategy which recognises and encourages employees to develop behaviours that match the intentions lying behind these changes is a major challenge.

The role of managers is changing too. They have become enablers and coaches rather than supervisors, and their skill now is to deliver consistently high performance in an environment based on trust. Rewarding performance in this environment has become more complex. Pay systems now also have to reflect the need to reward and reinforce teamworking skills as well as individual initiative. The 'how' of performance must be considered along with the 'what'. Demonstrating competencies and achieving results go hand in hand in successful organisations – as our case-studies show.

So is pay now more strategic?

Leading organisations with well developed HR strategies recognise that getting the best out of people today is not just about motivation and effort. Much more important is the fact that very few people reach their full potential and, in the past, too little attention was given to the development of the particular competencies needed by organisations. You either had what it took for progression and promotion or you stayed where you were. Employer attitudes to training are changing, encouraged among other things by the Investors in People initiative.

Change of this sort has already taken root at top executive level. Incentive scheme design using 'balanced scorecard' thinking on performance measures (ie related not just to profit or sales but also to service levels and the achievement of innovation, for example) and linked to the longer-term business strategy is all about the closest possible alignment between what executives do and what they get paid for. Further down the organisation competencies are being used both to define agreed performance levels and as an integral part of performance management and reward. More generally, organisations are building their values into reward communicators and drawing the definition of reward itself much broader than just pay.

As a result, the gap between integrated HR/reward policies of major employers and the basic administration of small firms is widening daily. This must be a major concern in an environment where much of the looked-for economic growth has come from small and medium-sized enterprises (SMEs).

Understanding the developing contribution of pay to people management

If the principal changes in organisations relate to structure, competence and cultural change, the ability to develop pay systems which can cope with this multiplicity of design criteria is not easy to acquire. But transparency remains vitally important: we already know that complex reward systems rarely motivate. The same is true of management. Understanding how the approach to pay has changed over the years helps us appreciate some of the problems we currently face.

Looking back at pay and bargaining arrangements is often instructive; those who do not learn from history are destined to repeat it. Traditional payment-by-results systems were often highly complex, but they were understood on the ground and worked as relatively crude encouragements to high volume production (and low cunning in beating the system). Time rates and salaries provided little incentive to work hard, so putting the emphasis on management's ability to organise and inspire. Traditional incremental scales had a logic based on recognising the improvement of performance which came with long service over a period of time from the committed majority. Job evaluation techniques helped to provide a degree of fairness in setting and managing relativities between different jobs, particularly for those engaged in non-manual work. Collective bargaining provided the channel for amendments to piece and pay rates and to job evaluation and pay systems, but also emphasised what employees, through their representatives, would settle for rather than what their organisations needed. And in fairly tight but growing labour markets this ensured that employers could keep their pay rates broadly in line so that they could pick up skills as and when they wanted them.

In the last ten years thinking on pay has changed enormously; the business agenda means it will change further. Quality, customer care and continuous improvement to product, process and service have come to depend on the effectiveness of systems of people management, including methods of pay.

From paying for output to paying for contribution

Performance pay was to some extent 'rediscovered' in the 1980s as part of the Thatcher 'economic revival'. The appeal, of course, was the simplistic and apparently equitable concept of the effort/reward economic contract.

Performance-related pay was typically linked rather mechanistically to annual performance appraisal/management systems based on output-focused objectives, and tended to involve comparatively small amounts of pay for all but those at the very top. The 'what' of performance mattered more than the 'how', which was considered too subjective and hard to identify. Performance-related pay often failed to build in important organisational values such as teamwork, taking acceptable risks, creativity and innovation. The reality that motivating the 'engine room' of the 70 to 80 per cent of people matters at least as much as rewarding the high achievers has taken time to surface in a world that originally saw greater value in focusing only on 'star' performers – who would always do all right anyway.

As time goes on, organisations are refining their approaches to performance-related pay. Performance appraisal has been a particular weakness and they are now radically rethinking performance management as a continuous, core management process by moving away from *rating* performance to *raising* performance. Performance-related pay does have a place, but more as a support than as a lever.

Paying to mould behaviour

Organisations which operate in more complex markets rely on employees' knowledge and their experience of customers and systems. They appreciate the length of time it can take to recruit, induct and bring a new employee 'up to speed', so they tend to look to their existing workforce to fill vacancies and seek to develop the people they have rather than recruiting people from outside – a different concept from the paternalism that once infused 'blue chip' company or public sector employment. Pay systems in such organisations are now geared to the reward, retention and motivation, but not the gratuitous 'feather-bedding', of employees. As we explain in Chapter 3, reward now contributes to the 'psychological contract' between employer and employee and can be a source of competitive advantage.

Some challenges

Ensuring consistency and fairness in pay outcomes will, in this new environment, remain probably the greatest challenge of all. But as pay becomes more individually orientated, reflecting the contribution of different people in different ways, pay structures could become less clear. Therein lies the challenge. Moving from the 1980s concept of equal opportunities with its emphasis on avoiding discrimination, to the newer, 'diversity'-based approaches currently emerging in the USA, will add complexity to pay thinking.

Meanwhile, existing 'equal pay for work of equal value' legislation is with us, but this is legislation drafted and enacted for a disappearing work environment. To deliver fairness among diverse employee groups is as much about mission, values and levels of trust as it is about compliance with the law.

Strategic partnerships, outsourcing, facilities management and related developments introduce the wider point about relationships between pay in major customer organisations and their suppliers. While the concept of a unified pay system within organisations can be key, the idea of the vertically integrated organisation has become less important. The relationship between pay in 'sun and satellite' organisations is currently being regulated by contract prices rather than directly by pay relationships, and the opening-up of substantial gaps in earnings relativities (and differentials) could have social as well as employee relations implications. The danger increases the more major organisations downsize and outsource activities. Self-regulation within, and regulation between, organisations will become important as they get down to the serious business of managing long-term relationships. Allowing extreme distortions of earnings differentials for jobs of similar responsibility and function could provoke a political intervention which would in turn make the management of reward within organisations much more difficult.

A similar set of arguments applies to pay determination in relation to the international labour market. Trade is becoming more open and competition on a labour cost basis is fierce. Increasingly, earnings can only be justifiable on the basis of the skills and flexibility of labour forces in one country as against others. The 'economic tigers' of the Pacific rim are competing hard across the whole spectrum of business. Even for the UK public services, software is being developed in India and document entry into computers is being done in Sri Lanka. Of course, labour rates in the developing world are increasing rapidly and at some point, perhaps, rates will converge. But that point is some way off yet and for the foreseeable future, and as long as trade continues to become more liberal, competition on labour rates will continue to provide the only competitive escape route for many organisations.

CHAPTER THREE

How Do We Think about Pay?

Ken Mayhew, Peter Ingram and David Guest

The influences on our thinking about pay come from many sources – economic, sociological and psychological as well as from management writers and gurus. This chapter outlines key influences. It does not attempt to be prescriptive, but provides an analytical framework which practitioners should find useful when developing pay strategies for their own individual purposes. First the major economic considerations are covered: the macro-economic constraints and influences; the degree of competition within the relevant labour market; and principal agent theory. Then two of the key management theories are discussed. Finally motivational theories are considered. These different angles of approach are not necessarily (or even usually) mutually exclusive. Often they come to similar conclusions from different disciplinary perspectives, but they are generally easier to understand if dealt with separately.

The macro-economic perspective

Macro-economists see labour services as important because they represent a substantial element in the total costs of production. Although direct expenditure on labour as a proportion of total expenditure varies considerably between firms, when the labour component of bought-in goods and services is included in company cost structures, the link between nominal wage growth and domestic price inflation becomes apparent. Concern about this is central to the maintenance of the Treasury's inflation target and the wish enunciated by successive Chancellors of the Exchequer to avoid a return to the perennial British problem of a wage/price spiral.

Since the second half of 1992, pay settlements, earnings and unit wage costs have sustained a moderate trend not seen since the mid-1960s. Over the same period retail price inflation has remained low. There are various possible explanations for these developments: first, the operation of the employment market may have become more flexible; second, the dominance of price competition across the economy may have prevented companies from passing on cost increases in price rises; and finally, the labour market has been recovering from the longest recession since the early 1930s. Each of these macro-economic factors is likely to have played its part in containing wage inflation in recent years.

Macro-economists are much concerned with the impact of economic cycles on pay. As the British economy moves through the second half of the 1990s, after four years of recovery the possibility of wage/price pressures again becomes the focus of attention. Over the last ten years economic relationships within the labour market have shifted. How does the situation in the second half of the 1990s compare with the previous economic cycle and how real is the threat of renewed inflation in the labour market as the economy grows? There are a number of warning signs. Unemployment has fallen by over 900,000 since the beginning of 1993. Over the last four years the growth of output per employee (productivity) across the economy as a whole increased from 1.2 per cent to nearly 4 per cent per annum before falling back again. Meanwhile the rate of price inflation increased from 1.2 per cent per year in mid-1993 to 3.5 per cent in mid-1995 and had dropped to 2.1 per cent by mid-1996.

The labour market response in the latter half of the 1990s differs from the post-1982–83 experience. Progressive deregulation has given management a freer hand in decisions affecting increases in the paybill. The fall in unemployment and the growth in employment has responded very rapidly to the recovery in GDP. By contrast, after the recession of the early 1980s the upturn in output at the beginning of 1982 was not followed by growth in employment until mid-1983. Unemployment began to fall only from early 1987, a lag of 14 quarters. This more immediate turnaround in the fortunes of the labour market in the 1990s is frequently cited as strong evidence of a structural shift or of greater flexibility.

This suggests that we are in a different environment from what has gone before. However, the challenge for management is no less severe because of this. Pay levels are fashioned both by comparisons within the firm and in the market place, and by individual and corporate performance. The market for labour is a very interdependent one (see below). Comparisons can exert considerable pressure for similar remuneration across similar types of labour. In this way supply and demand in each subsection of the labour market are brought into equilibrium. A competitive labour market is one where pay is determined by recruitment and retention rates across each occupational category. But pay is also used to reward effort and increased performance among individuals or across groups of employees. Where pay increases and levels are driven by improving performance, high performing companies can exert an upward influence, via comparability, on other firms.

The increased discipline of price competition in the late

1990s will make the balance between the use of pay as a managerial tool in promoting performance and the pressure of comparison more exacting than before. As the economy continues to grow, organisations must continue to recruit and retain capable employees. The future growth in productivity and the commercial demands of the workplace will require that these employees remain sufficiently motivated to work flexibly and effectively. Therefore, pay has to be used to seek to reward increased productivity and performance. However, the pay decisions made at each individual workplace will not be made in isolation. Comparisons with the size of wage awards made elsewhere or with the prevailing rate of price inflation will exert a strong influence on recruitment and retention rates. Managing such pressures and containing costs in a more competitive environment will be the principal feature of pay determination in the latter half of the 1990s.

Although the decline of the power of trade unions means that many employers may have a freer hand than in the past, the interdependencies in the market for labour services will mean that in many respects the problem remains as great as has been faced in the past. Indeed in one respect the difficulties of correctly managing the relationship between pay, employment and performance are likely to be more acute than before. This is because of the unprecedented external discipline from price competition. Managers will need to achieve a careful balance between the commercial demands of the competitive product market and avoiding the risks of breeding disaffected personnel. We return to this theme in the final chapter.

How competitive is your labour market?

There is no such thing as a single national labour market. Each employer operates in particular segments of the broader labour market which to varying degrees are insulated by, for example, occupation or geographical location. An important question for organisations considering pay strategy is just how competitive is the particular bit of the market in which they are operating. The simplest way of thinking about this is to ask how constrained you are in the pay levels currently being offered, and why you think this is. Classical economic theory tells us that it is the supply response of workers which dictates how binding such constraints will be. If a firm is not paying enough, then workers will attempt to obtain jobs with alternative employers. This response will be stronger, and the constraints therefore bigger, the more information workers have about alternative prospects and the smaller the perceived costs (both monetary and 'psychic') of moving jobs. Importantly, relevant information includes not just knowing about current offers from different prospective employers, but also how much is known about future prospects in different firms. Mobility costs are not just the expense of residential relocation, but can be quite substantial simply because of changed travel patterns within the same town, and because of psychological factors such as losing friends at work, moving children between schools, or sacrificing a familiar environment for an unfamiliar one. Also of importance is the way that higher-paying employers will react to the attempts of workers to obtain employment with their firms. Classical theory would suggest that such attempts should encourage them to reduce rewards. Conversely, lower-paying firms should be forced to push up their pay in order to retain and recruit staff. However, this equalising process is likely to be stopped in its tracks if sufficient high-paying employers acted according to the so-called 'efficiency wage' hypothesis. This hypothesis indicates that they would resist the bidding down process for reasons of 'adverse selection' and of 'moral hazard'. Adverse selection refers to the possibility that some of a high-paying employer's existing workers might leave if they had wage cuts or freezes imposed upon them. They could be replaced, but the likelihood is that their replacements would be less effective employees. Moral hazard refers to the adverse morale and motivation effects suffered by the workers who remain after the pay cuts or freezes.

Also important for determining the degree to which a firm is insulated from external market forces is the extent to which workers in a firm have 'specific' skills or attributes. If an employee receives training which leads to a skill which is specific – ie usable only by the employer with whom that skill is acquired – then the worker is in part removed from the external market. Imagine, for example, that someone is hired who is worth £100 to the hiring firm and to other firms in the market. The employer then trains the individual, so that this worth rises to £150. If the skill is specific, the worker will still be worth only £100 elsewhere. This gives the employer the discretion to pay such an employee anywhere within the range £100 to £150. By contrast if the skill acquired is a general one, then the employer has no such discretion, since the worker will also be worth £150 elsewhere. Clearly 'specific' and 'general' skills are at extreme ends of a continuum, and most skills lie somewhere between these two extremes. Yet the example is illustrative of the circumstances that will prevail if some degree of specificity is involved. In fact a sort of bilateral monopoly has developed. Put crudely, the worker is one of a limited number of people who, in the short run, can provide a particular skill, while the employer is the only person who demands it. Today's employers are much concerned to 'match' their employees to the firm. This is evident in the hiring process and also in the process of in-company induction and personal development. Analytically, such matching has the same impact as the presence of specific skills. When forces such as the above exist, economists describe workers as being in 'internal labour markets'. Their attachment to the labour market outside their current firm is relatively weak. The key conclusion to this section is that the presence of an internal labour market gives the employer greater ability to make decisions about pay without worrying about external pressures. However, it does pose awkward problems in a world where it is said that lifetime employment with one employer is disappearing.

Principal agent theory

'Principal agent' theory has had a major impact on economic thinking and lies behind much of what we hear from general (ie non-HRM) commentary on the effort/reward relationship. Principal agent theory started with a simple insight and has rapidly developed to stimulate a massive amount of academic work, much of it of considerable technical complexity. It has been employed primarily by industrial economists, but it is also widely used by labour economists (particularly in the USA). A few simple examples of the approach are described below in order to illustrate how it has formed a framework for thinking about pay.

The *principal* is the manager and the *agents* are the workers. The interests of the two parties are not coincident. The 'utility' of the worker depends positively on pay and negatively on 'effort', where effort represents not just sweat of the brow but (for instance) allocating time as effectively between different tasks or functions as management would want. The 'utility' of the manager depends negatively on pay of staff and positively on their effort. If effort is observable, then there is no problem. The manager can set up an incentive/punishment structure which (suitably calibrated) will bring forth the appropriate amount of effort. Problems start to occur when effort is not directly observable. Even then matters may be relatively straightforward if output or results are measurably related to effort. In this case the manager simply calibrates the punishment/incentive structure against output, confident that this will elicit the appropriate effort. Things start to get difficult either when output is not observable or when it is observable but depends not only on effort but on (so-called) 'state of the world variables' over which the employee has no control; both are common in the public sector.

It may come as some surprise to personnel professionals to find that the mainstream literature tends not to stress the case where output is unobservable. This is wrong, and the issue will be returned to later. Instead the literature concentrates on the case where it is impossible to disentangle the relative effects of effort and 'state of the world' variables on output. It is easy to demonstrate that under such circumstances a straightforward payment by results (PBR) system of any description loses much of its appeal. Under PBR the employees are required to share risk – if output falls because of adverse movements in 'state of the world' variables, then their pay is affected by factors outside their control. If employees are risk-averse, the downside of this will weigh more heavily with them than the upside. In the end they will demand compensation for bearing such risk, and thus any given level of output will cost more than otherwise. Cost escalation prompts the search for an alternative method of extracting effort.

Generically there are three broad alternatives. The first is organisational change which might itself alter the nature of the incentives on offer. The second is more extensive monitoring of employee performance. The third is an alternative payments system.

Individual merit or performance pay is one such alternative. The argument goes as follows. Take a group of employees who, management believe, are affected similarly by 'state of the world' variables. Although we cannot disentangle the absolute impact of such variables an any individual employee's output or results, each person in the group is affected similarly. Thus differences in their performance will reflect differences in their effort, and rewarding by relative performance thus makes sense.

Ironically, principal agent theory can be used with equal conviction to suggest a very different solution. We have the same problem of asymmetric information – ie employees know more about their own efforts than do employers. Employers can adopt the following tactic. They accept that most of the time employees will go undetected if they cheat or chisel. However, employers reason that just occasionally, and perhaps only once, an individual's cheating will be detected. Then the harshest penalty will be incurred – dismissal. In order to make the penalty even harsher, pay will be deferred. The idea is represented in Figure 7, which displays the time profiles of an individual's earnings and productivity under such a scheme. Essentially it shows that an individual is paid less than he or she is worth in the early years with the firm, and more

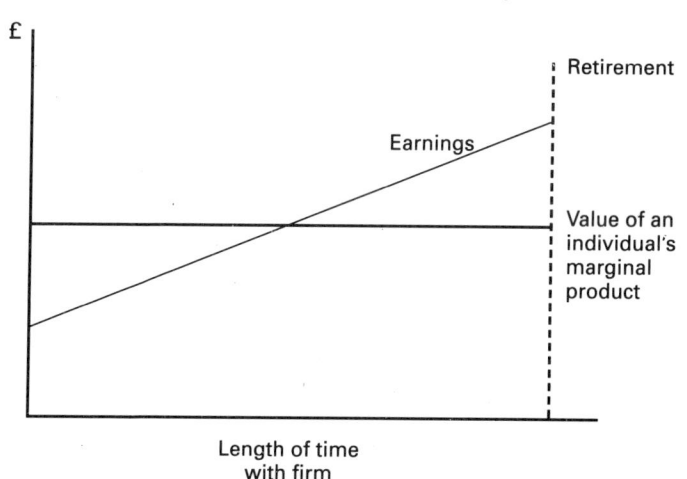

Figure 7 *Earnings and productivity*

than he or she is worth in later years. Thus it is as if the employee is posting a bond of good behaviour. If caught cheating, the individual not only loses the job but also forfeits the bond. This is known as the deferred compensation model, or more fondly, to managers of an older generation, as seniority pay. Of course, in order for such a scheme to work, an internal labour market has to exist, and so there will be many circumstances when it is simply inappropriate. By contrast, the use of merit pay is not so obviously dependent on internalisation.

In this simple form, principal agent theory embraces a relatively poverty-stricken view of what constitutes human motivation. Thus we go on to consider a variety of managerial, sociological and psychological approaches. However, principal agent theory does demonstrate that apparently powerful arguments for one system of payment can provide an equally compelling case for a very different system. Without greater knowledge of the particular characteristics of the employees involved, and of the firm that employs them, no decisively general case can be made.

Motivation theory

Historically there have been three major psychological approaches to pay and motivation. *Individual need theories* are associated predominantly with Maslow and Herzberg. Maslow, as many management students of the last 20 years will remember, outlined a hierarchy of needs in which the role of pay was uncertain but it was not the highest level of need – a place occupied by self-actualisation. Herzberg's motivator-hygiene theory distinguished between 'extrinsic' or 'hygiene' factors (eg working conditions, supervision and job security) and 'motivators' or 'intrinsic' factors (eg interest, challenge and the exercise of responsibility).

Extrinsic factors, he argued, had little or no effect on positive satisfaction, determining only whether someone was dissatisfied or not. It was intrinsic factors which determined positive job satisfaction. Herzberg classified pay as a 'hygiene' factor. Critical review of his work questions Herzberg's analysis from his own research evidence – the current view is that pay has some motivational value as long as it is perceived as fair.

Orientations theory was adapted by sociologists from the ideas of psychologists. Orientations to work are persistent personal values that people develop through socialisation at home, school and the community. They shape the sorts of things that people look for in a job and that they are likely to find motivating. The implication is that there are quite large differences in individual preferences and therefore in how employees respond to management initiatives and attempts to motivate them. A number of writers in this tradition emphasised the existence of 'instrumental' workers who saw work purely as a means to an end and who therefore valued high pay. Later work uncovered far more diversity than this. It stressed that workers gravitate to the sort of work that most matches their needs. Thus, a premium is put on careful selection which would ensure that a firm had workers who would respond consistently and predictably to management initiatives.

In sum, the above theories suggest that needs and orientations are largely fixed outside the workplace, giving pay a limited role in altering these deep-seated attitudes. The emphasis is rather on being careful about the type of worker selected – ie the qualities of the job and person matching.

Reinforcement theory and behaviour modification ignores needs and concentrates on behaviour. Specifically, it is concerned with what 'carrots and sticks' can modify behaviour. The critical starting point is learning theory, and a distinction between learning (or the acquisition of knowledge and skills) and performance (or the translation of knowledge and skills into practice). To influence performance, action could be taken on the 'antecedents' (for example, exhortation, guidance, promises) and/or on the consequences (rewards, punishments and feedback). Behaviour modification argues that it is better to focus on the consequences rather than on the antecedents.

Of course, this would seem to assign a critical role to pay, but the approach recognises that different people will react differently to any given pay incentive. Other reinforcers include promotion, a better choice of future activities and projects, recognition and praise, awards and straightforward information on quality, sales or service improvement.

So the choice of the appropriate reward structure is not as easy as it seems at first sight; nor is the identification of the performance to reward. One can, for instance, observe an obvious tendency to reward the short-term and the visible rather than the long-term and the less easily measured. A third difficulty is to devise the appropriate mechanism for delivering the rewards. Research clearly shows that behaviour modification does alter behaviour. However, it also shows that the wrong things and the wrong people are often rewarded.

The central shortcoming of behaviour modification theory is its failure to give sufficient weight to the social context and to the way in which individuals actively interpret their environment rather than acting as passive recipients of, and respondents to, stimuli and rewards. Expectancy theory attempts to fill part of this gap by building a social dimension into motivation.

Expectancy theory is probably the most useful motivation theory for the consideration of pay. It is different from the other approaches we have outlined in being what is described as a cognitive theory. This means that motivation is based on what we expect to happen and upon our perceptions of our environment rather than on inner needs or on reinforcement of direct personal experience. According to expectancy theory, motivation is a function of the link between perceptions of effort, performance and reward. Effort is likely to be forthcoming only if you believe that there is a link between your effort and performance and between your performance, and your reward. Modern versions of expectancy theory in addition stress that performance is strongly influenced by ability, motivation and role perception; ie an understanding of what behaviour is required to be successful in a particular role. It also distinguishes between levels of reward. Performing a task may be valued in itself or it may be a means to an end. Earning money may be an end in itself or it may be a means to an end – increased power in the organisation, status or purchasing power, for example. The theory works best in clearly defined settings and where there are significant decisions to take, rather than routine everyday ones. It works less well under narrowly defined conditions than does a more tightly specified approach such as goal-setting.

Expectancy theory and principal agent theory are clearly closely linked. The former adds behavioural richness to the stark analytical content of the latter. So a useful framework for thinking about pay might be a synthesis of the two; but before outlining the implications of such a synthesis, we examine some of the empirical evidence about the effectiveness of various incentive systems.

The evidence

Unfortunately, but not surprisingly, the evidence on the impact of the different types of incentive payment systems discussed in this chapter is inconclusive. However, many studies (more American than British) do find the following common problems with individual incentive/merit pay systems.

- The assessment method may be faulty. Nickell[3] cites two pieces of American evidence. Two assessors of the same employees gave rankings with a correlation of, at best, only 0.6 (King *et al.*) In a study by Hunter the correlation between an assessor's rating and an alternative measure of performance was 0.4 for a sample of civilian jobs and 0.27 for a sample of military jobs.
- 'Rating drift' can easily occur. For example, it is hard to maintain the same rating for people who perform well year after year. Rating is itself proving to be a reward, especially in times of low inflation and modest pay progression.
- There is a risk of deterioration of morale among those who are rated low relative to their own expectations. These effects are especially marked where unfairness or inconsistency are perceived.
- Returning to a point made earlier, the very difficulty of measuring output or results may be reflected in the problems listed above. It might also result in a misallocation of time. For example, attempts to set measurable output-related targets may actually omit important core elements of a person's job, where speed of response, customer service, quality of problem-solving and analytical thinking are important. In this category fall lawyers, research scientists, policy-makers in government, flight attendants, nurses and many other specialist groups.

A number of American and British writers find it difficult to discern positive effects of performance pay on various measures of organisational performance. On Britain, see, for example, Marsden and Richardson (1994)[4] on the Inland Revenue, and Thompson (1992)[5] on a sample of public and private sector organisations. More positive recent evidence comes from an analysis of the 1990 Workplace Industrial Relations Survey by Fernie, Metcalf and Woodland (1994)[6]. They find that 'contingent payment systems' (which can include anything from individual merit pay through group incentives to profit sharing) have a positive impact on workplace productivity. However, the case is a difficult one to prove. There are so many other factors affecting a company's performance which are difficult to disentangle from a particular method of reward.

Thus the evidence is not clinching either way on whether individual performance pay schemes work; similarly for group or corporate schemes. However, as Nickell shows, American empirical work reveals some interesting issues. It suggests a more discernible productivity effect for schemes involving groups or sections or divisions. This, Nickell argues, implies that 'free rider' effects are more than offset by 'co-operation' effects. Free rider effects refer to the phenomenon whereby members of a group believe that the lack of their own contribution will not be missed and their consequent belief that they can rely on others to put in the effort to produce the results, but still share in the rewards attached to those results. By contrast, the evidence on company-wide schemes (eg profit sharing or ESOPs) is less strong, though sometimes positive productivity effects are found. Nickell suggests that the free rider effects are potentially much stronger here, and that to be successful, company-wide schemes have to be accompanied by what he calls 'substantive participation' (for which autonomy is essential), long-term employment and guaranteed employment rights.

What can we learn from the theories?

We have suggested that a synthesis of principal agent

theory with expectancy theory is a productive approach.

The key implications of this synthesis are as follows:

- Reward policy should link effort to performance, and performance to reward.
- There should be attractive and significant rewards available which clearly outweigh any costs perceived to be involved in pursuing them, such as threats to job security.
- Perceptions about the attractiveness of rewards and about the links between effort, performance and reward are derived from the social context and are therefore capable of being influenced.
- It is essential to be able to define performance and to assess it in ways that are broadly acceptable. For example, does the organisation wish to reward adequate or exceptional performance? Or is it possible or appropriate to attempt to identify individual performance in an organisation which relies on group working? Or is there a danger that in an attempt to measure performance, attention is focused on what is easily measurable at the expense of more intangible but more important issues? Or, and this is especially true in banks, building societies and customer-focused Government agencies, do *consistent* levels of service-defined performance matter more than performance distributions which need to be kept to the minimum?
- Motivation will have an impact on performance only if care is taken to ensure that employees have the necessary knowledge and skills, and that they understand their role, what is expected of them, and what they have to do to obtain the rewards.
- Perceptions of fairness are of vital importance.
- Openness is also important if fairness is to be perceived.
- Both expectancy theory and principal agent theory are future-orientated. They suggest that effort will be

expended now in the expectation of future rewards. This implies either very straightforward immediate rewards, tied in to performance, or a very high level of trust. Particularly at managerial and professional levels, where short-term rewards are less practicable, the organisational culture must be one which supports the 'faith' that the implied promises will be delivered. In a world of rapid change and one in which the traditional psychological contract between company and manager is evolving as long-term careers become less feasible, the ability to maintain this kind of trust may become more difficult.
- There are many rewards other than pay. People concerned with pay policy should step back and reflect on the relative importance of pay compared with other rewards as well as the size of any incentive if it is to have an influence on motivation.
- To the extent that pay is thought to be an important tool, the precise functional purpose of any payments system should be carefully defined.
- The degree to which a group of workers is internalised, as opposed to being externally market-oriented, will be important in determining the range of options available to management.
- The nature of the production process is of vital importance, in particular whether it is team-based or not.

Conclusion

When setting pay, all managers are constrained to some extent by the external market. In using pay as a managerial tool to encourage and reward performance they can never ignore this constraint. At the same time the effectiveness of any particular approach to rewards is critically dependent on the nature of the employees concerned, on the job they do, on the product or service they are involved in producing, and on organisational design and culture. The aim of this chapter has been to suggest in which ways the different thinking about how both the external and internal constraints can be viewed and evaluated when considering decisions about pay levels and pay systems.

CHAPTER FOUR

The State of the Art in the Private Sector

Clive Wright

Where does all this take us? The discussion in previous chapters outlines the major business, economic, social and management issues, and their implications for pay and rewards. This chapter uses case-studies to identify some of the practical approaches that private sector companies have taken in changing their reward strategies to meet these challenges. In each case the strategies which are described have been developed only after careful consideration of business need and objectives, and taking into account the changes that have taken, and will take, place in the employee profile and environment. However, the development and implementation of any new strategy is not quick, simple or, generally, cheap. Organisations therefore need to be quite clear about the reasons for a new remuneration strategy *before* raising the concerns or expectations of employees by developing a new one.

In the late 1960s and the 1970s few companies expected to have a remuneration plan, let alone a strategy, covering the processes linking pay to employee motivation, performance and flexibility. Pay was generally an administrative issue. The industrial relations and consequent pay agendas were centrally driven and, as a result, the options open to companies were quite limited. The Donovan Report on

Trade Unions and Employers' Associations published in 1968 and Barbara Castle's white paper 'In Place of Strife' which followed it in 1969 were symptomatic of the centralist environment which existed in the late 1960s and which had a significant influence on remuneration thinking and practice. These were followed in the 1970s by double-figure inflation, economic decline and industrial strife, all of which encouraged an 'accountancy-based' approach to remuneration, based on 'across the board' negotiated increases, piecework or human asset/resource accounting systems. Remuneration during the 1960s and 1970s was about using systematic processes, such as job evaluation, to 'tidy up' previously chaotic pay relativities and fine-tuning pay administration and cost controls by using finely graded structures. It was primarily a control system. Remuneration was not seen as a strategic personnel tool.

The proportion of employees whose pay was fixed by joint negotiation in the 1960s ranged between 66 per cent of employees (*Industrial Relations Handbook* 1961, Ministry of Labour) to nearly 80 per cent if those covered by wage councils are included (Ministry of Labour submission to the Donovan Report 1968). By 1990 these figures had dropped to 54 per cent and 65 per cent respectively.

With the abolition of wage councils under the Trade Union Reform and Employee Rights Act 1993, which affected nearly 2.5 million employees, and the reduction in central pay bargaining, the percentage of employees covered by collective pay agreements is now lower than at any time since the end of the First World War.

The turning point for employers, employees and more or less everyone else, was probably the 'winter of discontent' in 1978, followed by the election of the Conservative Government in 1979. British industry clearly could not go on as before. Something significant had to change. Industrial relations had to be rebalanced, a sense of common purpose and social responsibility had to be engendered, and an environment of accountability had to be established.

As a result, organisations took back the managerial freedoms in which to develop their personnel and remuneration strategies. But research shows that not as many as might be expected are taking the opportunity to develop strategies that are appropriate and necessary to support the changes in their business.

Some organisations did respond immediately to the new environment. Others did not take advantage of it until the 1990s. As the focus groups held in April 1994 by a working group of the IPD as part of the early background research for this book showed, some companies have yet to grasp the opportunity to develop a business-focused personnel and remuneration strategy. This is even more surprising in that the range of remuneration 'tools' is probably more extensive now than at any other time.

Organisations now have much more freedom and opportunity to develop and use a remuneration strategy based upon business need – and they have the responsibility to do so. Some personnel people argue that they cannot develop remuneration strategies in their organisation because remuneration is always used tactically, but on closer examination it often turns out that remuneration is used tactically because there has never been a remuneration strategy or any pressure from either the board or the personnel department to introduce one. Without a clear view of the longer-term objectives, organisations will of course keep stumbling on from month to month, and year to year. To paraphrase Hamel and Prahalad (1994)[7] the vicious circle needs to become a virtuous circle.

Rod Kuipers, chief executive of DHL Worldwide Express, Europe and Africa, outlined four main criticisms that line managers had of personnel departments in an article in *People Management* (May 1995):

- Personnel departments develop over-complex plans and

systems that don't have a bearing on real business need.
- They don't know what is going on at the business front line.
- They cannot think strategically.
- There is a lack of concrete results from personnel.

This view is that the personnel function is usually a collection of technical HR functions, all presided over by an HR manager or director. 'What HR so often lacks is the ability to provide *practical* strategic input that chief executives and others can use.' (However, there is also the countervailing view, as a survey by the Management Centre Europe into business leadership shows, that many chief executives are also not as effective as they could be.)

One of the significant issues that affects the development and acceptance of a remuneration strategy is the lack of any pay literacy or competency among many managers – chief executives included. The popular misconception is that remuneration is simple. We are all motivated, we all perform well, we all get paid. Pay is a common phenomenon so where is the complexity in linking it all together? But if we take the economic issues and changing employment environment identified in Chapter 2, the complexities of the labour market and motivational theories outlined in Chapter 3, the need for any remuneration strategy to support the business objectives and to ensure a good 'fit' with the structure, capability and culture of the organisation, it very quickly becomes apparent that the development of a remuneration strategy is a complex balance of a range of priorities.

If those responsible for the approval or implementation of the strategy do not understand the problems, options and benefits that any proposal seeks to sort out, there is little possibility of its being successful, even if accepted. However, this does not absolve the personnel professional from proceeding with the development of a strategy, but it does mean that some management education is necessary before there is any hope of successfully implementing the final plan.

A recent report by consultants Towers Perrin (1994) on the utilities industries indicated HR strategy and policy development as the most important area for more businesses in the future. The utilities industries are not alone in this respect. There are many companies in traditional industries that have no strategic personnel or remuneration plan. There is therefore a clear need for professionals in personnel and in each elected function to develop and communicate a strategic plan. Personnel could be pushing at an open door because there is now a widespread realisation, with the change in the industrial environment, that remuneration is an important strategic business tool. So every chief executive, personnel manager and remuneration specialist must ask themselves whether they are clear on the remuneration strategy for their company. If not, why not, and what are they going to do about it?

The case-studies presented in this chapter are real examples of how leading companies in the private sector have developed their remuneration strategies on an integrated basis with HR management in the face of a variety of challenges. However, they are examples; they are not proposed as models. The strategies outlined here have been developed based upon *their* businesses and *their* personnel strategies. It is extremely unlikely that exactly the same circumstances will apply elsewhere. Approaches to pay strategy development differ, and no single pay strategy will deliver the motivations and behaviours that organisations need to succeed in the 1990s. So, read and learn – but treat with care.

Remuneration management strategies are characterised by diversity and conditioned by both the legacy of the past and the realities of the present. Every organisation can learn from these examples of how it has been done in other companies, and apply the same thinking and development processes to understand their business and to develop the remuneration strategy for their own organisation.

As a nation we have to take this opportunity to use remuneration to make a positive contribution to our competitive effectiveness in the global market-place.

ICL PLC

> The first case-study shows how ICL had to introduce a new business strategy in the face of a variety of challenges. It outlines the personnel management aspects of that strategy, and the role of pay in the overall plan. The case-study covers the moves to a performance culture in the 1980s, and the more recent steps to build on that by giving equal weight to skills development.

Background

ICL has a long history in the information technology industry which can be traced back to 1904 when The Tabulator Ltd company was formed to manufacture and market Hermann Hollerith's punch-card machines. ICL itself, was formed by a Government-initiated merger of International Computers and Tabulators and English Electric in 1968. It is a company which has always been involved in mergers and acquisitions, most recently with Nokia Data Systems in 1991 which doubled the number of employees in continental Europe.

In 1979, as part of Margaret Thatcher's policy of Government disengagement from direct involvement in industry, the Government sold off its minority shareholding in ICL. At that time the company was very successful, with annual turnover up by 23 per cent and profit increased by 22 per cent.

However, in 1980 there was a dramatic change in the company's fortunes. A rise in the exchange rate affected overseas orders, the UK economy went into recession and a price war between IBM and the plug-compatible mainframe manufacturers caused a sharp reduction in profit margins. By 1981 the company was losing money and needed to be supported by a loan guarantee from the Government. This crisis resulted in a change in senior management and a series of significant cost-cutting measures. Between 1980 and 1985 the headcount was reduced from 33,000 to 20,000 employees, although by 1982 the company was back in profit. It is against this background that the new management undertook a fundamental review of the company's strategy, with the development of a new personnel strategy as one of the key outcomes.

Personnel strategy development

Until this time ICL had been primarily a mainframe supplier, enjoying a level of support from the Government through a favourable purchasing policy. The development of mid-range computers, and the open, competitive tendering policy introduced by the Conservative Government increased the need to be commercially competitive and to focus on employee productivity. The new personnel strategy therefore had to concentrate on moving the business:

from	to
Technology-led	Business-led
UK focus	International growth (especially Europe)
Managers doing	Managers managing
Hours worked	Performance-focused
Capacity-led	Market-led
Union-negotiated increases	Performance-related rewards
Local projects	Total quality

Company culture

Overriding this strategy was the necessity for a major change in the culture of the company. The new management of ICL therefore undertook a number of initiatives including:

- a high-profile communication of the new business strategy by the managing director.
- development, in conjunction with the London Business School, of a new management training programme for all employees between first line management and senior executive – the Core Management Programme
- publication of a booklet called *The ICL Way* which detailed the employee obligations and management requirements which would form the basis of the new company culture and values
- formal performance reviews, both business and individual
- organisation and management development reviews at all levels.

In order to underpin and reinforce the cultural changes, a new remuneration strategy was developed which was to have a significant impact on ICL's ability to manage change in the future.

UK remuneration strategy development – performance-related pay

Until 1982 the company had recognised a number of unions for pay bargaining, job evaluation, health and safety, grievance and disciplinary purposes in the UK. Discussions on pay had always been based around the across-the-board increase (usually RPI plus) with the company awarding a further small discretionary percentage for merit at a later date. At this time there were clear delineations between the manual workers (who were unionised, paid weekly, and with different terms and conditions of employment), the technical and professional workers (some of whom, while unionised, were paid monthly with different terms and conditions of employment) and managers (who were mainly non-unionised and had better terms and conditions of employment).

With the new strategy of performance management and the need to focus as much of the pay increase as possible on reward for performance, ICL set the objective of introducing merit-related pay, with or without trade union support. However, it was clear this would not be reasonable or realistic until managers had been able to demonstrate that the performance of employees would be reviewed objectively, against criteria that were related to the business needs. The company therefore began to develop personal objectives with every employee, (including the production workers in manufacturing) linked to the business plans. These would be the measures of successful performance achievement. It was important that the objectives were developed *with* the employee in order to give a higher level of commitment to the achievement of those objectives. These were then reviewed regularly by the manager and employee, and the level of achievement of the objectives agreed.

The most important of these objectives were used as some of the measures in the management bonus plan that was introduced. Financial targets were also used in order to support the focus on measurement and achievement, which was a key requirement of the performance management programme. This combination of financial and personal objectives ensured that there was a balanced measure between the annual and longer-term objectives of the company.

During the same period the performance appraisal process was modified so that it became less of a 'tick box' approach and required managers to discuss with employees the behavioural characteristics that they exhibited (good and bad) in the performance of their normal jobs. The agreement on the employee's abilities then led to the development of the training and career plans.

This change in the process of setting objectives and appraising employees required a significant effort in training. The training was incorporated into the Core Management Programme and also made up a specific course for those who had already undergone basic management training. This commitment to training has been a fundamental tenet of ICL over many years.

At the same time the company initiated and developed an Employee Opinion Survey. As is fairly normal these days, the survey contained many questions about the overall working environment, but also covered objective setting and appraisal process. After two years or so, when the Employee Opinion Survey showed that employees thought the appraisal process to be reasonably fair, ICL notified the union that the pay award in 1986 would be on an all-merit basis. Not surprisingly the unions were not happy about this, but a ballot of members decided that they would not take industrial action to resist the proposal. This was probably the first occasion since the Company's founding that ICL had a truly performance-related pay system. To do it, they needed:

- commitment and support from the very top of the company
- a clear statement of the company's business objectives
- training for managers and employees throughout the company
- well-developed personal objectives
- a supportive, open appraisal system

- all pay increases to be based upon merit.

In order to support the company's need to motivate all employees to play their part in an ever more competitive business environment, ICL decided in 1988 to harmonise the terms and conditions of employment and benefits for all blue- and white-collar workers and include them on the general grading structure with the same salary scales and benefits. While the company readily concedes that this entailed an increase in operating costs at a time when it could not be readily afforded, it has enabled it to have a more flexible and committed workforce with a higher level of productivity.

Underlying all these changes was a new management style, which was much more open and approachable; and management took positive steps through better communications, establishing quality circles and setting up TQM systems to involve the employees in the business.

Checking progress

After a number of years of running the Employee Opinion Survey, which every year included general questions of employee satisfaction on pay and benefits, the Manager – Group Remuneration decided that a special survey was required to identify any issues and to provide feedback on employees' views of the remuneration processes and the benefits package. After much internal debate over the procedure to be used, the questions that could be included, and how the results were to be analysed and used, structured interviews were held with 200 employees in August 1991. The employees were randomly selected but represented the characteristics of the general employee population. The results showed that :

- 91.5 per cent of employees generally agreed with their manager's appraisal of their performance.
- There was an issue over the level of discussion between the manager and employee about pay decisions.
- Only 14.5 per cent rated their earnings as unfavourable (and very few had any idea about which companies they thought paid higher than ICL).
- Although 75 per cent of respondents felt that the benefits package fitted their needs, 40 per cent thought that the communication on benefits needed improving.
- Although the pay levels were generally seen as reasonable, and most agreed with their manager's view of their performance, 31 per cent of respondents thought that the company was not doing a very good job in matching pay to performance.

Further investigation showed that managers still felt (despite there now being no union-negotiated, across-the-board increase) that they were restricted in the amount they could give as pay increases and in the distribution of increases between employees. The steps that the company took to overcome this are described later.

In the meantime, in the light of the comments in the survey ICL decided that further work was needed to explain to employees how their remuneration and benefits package was made up and what they could do individually to influence their progression and therefore level of pay. It had been publishing an annual employee pension benefit statement for several years, but the content had been specifically on pensions, and the format less than exciting. The first action it took to improve employee understanding was to include all the benefits in the statement and to personalise it and make it as comprehensive and interesting as possible. In March 1992, ICL published its first employee booklet on pay and benefits. This was given to every employee at the time of their annual pay review so that they had a clear idea of the factors influencing their pay. It was the first time that a clear statement had been given to them on how the job evaluation, grades, salary scales and the appraisal system were linked together, and what factors their manager took into account in determining individual salary increases. The major employee benefits were also included in the booklet to reinforce the message that the remuneration package was more than just pay.

Devolving pay decisions

After withdrawing from formal negotiations on pay with the unions at the corporate level, ICL had four major pay review dates – January for sales people; April for the senior executives in the company; June for production, clerical, technical and professional employees; and September for middle and senior managers. Each of these separate groups had its own salary increase budget which might be the same, but was often different. This meant that a manager could not balance the salary increases between groups and, for example, give low salary increases to the managers and give higher increases to the technical or clerical employees. Each group had a separate increase budget, and money could not be shifted between them. Also, while a great deal of consideration was given to deciding the salary increase level for each group, there was no overall measure of the level of salary increase for promotions, inequities or 'other' reasons during the year.

To overcome these issues the Corporate Remuneration Group developed a pay planning spreadsheet. This was developed in-house so that employee information could be downloaded from the personnel information system and, after the work was complete, could be loaded back into the system. An overall salary increase budget for *all* employees in 1991 was agreed by the board, and managers were required to plan all of the salary increases (merit, promotions, inequities, others, etc) for all their employees for the whole year, within the overall increase budget. This allowed managers to balance the levels of increase in the way that best reflected the performance of the people in the department. It also meant that it was not necessary to promote someone to give them a significantly higher increase – it was all within the one overall budget.

Because the salary increase plans for the UK were held centrally on the personnel information system, the overall level of increase and basis of distribution of the increase could be analysed centrally. This analysis was then reviewed by the board before approval was given for the plans. Managers could still adjust individual increases as they became due during the year, subject to normal approval processes, but the total increase budget could not be exceeded. This new process of devolved responsibility allowed managers much more control over the distribution of the agreed increase than before, and they soon began to take much more ownership of pay decisions.

However, while this gave freedom to distribute pay, it did not address the problem that some businesses and departments needed higher levels of increase than the average, and some might need less. This was not easily determined at a top level and therefore, as a further development of the devolution of pay decisions, the board agreed, but only on the basis of the successful programme so far, that individual businesses could decide what level of salary increase they needed overall and then determine how this would be distributed. An immediate concern for the personnel managers in the business divisions was that significant differences in increase budgets could lead to their losing key employees to other divisions that had higher levels of increase. The Corporate Remuneration Group was therefore asked to be information broker, and to approach any division that had an increase significantly different from the others. As it turned out, the sharing of information led to adjustments of increase levels so that most were in a small band. This further devolution of decisions on pay increases has led to more effective linking of pay to performance.

Throughout the period of the implementation of this strategy the IT industry has been in turmoil. The recent fantastic growth of the PC market, but the significant reduction in profit margins, has led to the major business problems so well documented for other IT companies. However, while ICL has not been immune to these pressures it has been able to fare better than almost all the other IT companies.

Developing the strategy for the future

The high level of commitment to a performance-related pay system has served ICL very effectively over the last ten years. However, the pressures on business margins, the need to streamline all processes, the reduction in management levels and a changing employee environment, which will be much more skills-led, is now leading to a change from a total focus on performance-related pay to an equal emphasis on the development of skills and capabilities. This is starting with a change in the people profile as the business plans are developed, and is being translated into specific skills and capability needs that the business requires. ICL is currently implementing processes to develop itself further as a learning organisation, more responsibility being passed to employees for the ownership of their own skill and capability development. To support this change in the focus of employee development the company is designing a structure of job families to replace the traditional individual job evaluation and salary scales.

These will help employees measure their progress, and also give managers a framework to measure the market 'worth' of employees in order to make pay decisions more effectively. This does not mean that the company is dropping its performance-related pay strategy – but it is shifting some of the emphasis on to the measure of capability as well. By rewarding employees who develop capabilities that clearly relate to the company's business needs, it hopes to strengthen, not weaken, its performance culture.

Whether the change is successful remains to be seen. The fact that ICL has been successful in the development of its remuneration strategy over a number of years suggests that it will.

MERCURY COMMUNICATIONS

> Mercury Communications was a fast-growing subsidiary of Cable and Wireless in the 1980s, but had to retrench because of fierce price competition. Flexibility has been a key feature of Mercury's pay philosophy and this case-study looks at the company's approach to flexible performance management approaches and benefits provision.

Background

Mercury Communications was set up in 1982 and was the first competitor in the telecommunications industry to challenge BT's monopoly. Owned by Cable and Wireless, which in 1992 sold a 20 per cent share to Bell Canada Enterprises, Mercury has grown rapidly in the last decade becoming a major player offering a full range of services to 12 per cent (by revenue) of the total UK telecommunications market. Mercury's annual turnover is over £1.5 billion. After a decade of rapid growth, during which

Mercury has offered a full portfolio of services including voice, data and imaging transmission, messaging, and premises equipment, and during which employee numbers have increased from 2,000 to well over 10,000, in 1994 Mercury announced a shift in its corporate strategy. They had to respond to major changes in the UK telecommunications market with the emergence of more than a hundred competitors offering telephony services, most of which have been competing on cost as well as targeting Mercury's main areas of business – international, large corporations and the City of London. The telecommunications industry reeled, if only temporarily, when in 1994, Mercury announced some retrenchment to a new headcount of 8,000 by the end of 1995 and a new move towards 'focus' and 'differentiation' between networks and products-and-services.

Employee environment

Mercury's approach to human resource management needs to be set against the context of rapid growth, a young workforce with relatively short service and no trade union representation for the purposes of bargaining on pay, terms and conditions. The functional breakdown in 1994 was as follows:-

	%
Engineers	38
Sales	14
Support (eg billing enquiries)	27
Other professionals	9
IT	7
Marketing	5

Mercury has some 80 locations throughout the UK. From its inception Mercury adopted and developed a culture of performance-linked pay at the level of the individual, against the backdrop of a fluid and flat organisational structure. The role of line management in the determination of pay levels was emphasised from the start. Mercury has never used traditional pay management techniques such as job evaluation, grades, or salary ranges, opting instead for an approach that places the key emphasis on external and internal market comparators, individual performance and the company's ability to pay. By definition, therefore, Mercury has a regional strategy with appropriate levels of pay within the appropriate functional or regional market. The corporate human resources team fully briefs line management across the business units by supplying detailed market analysis and 'roadshow' briefings.

Business imperatives for change

Mercury's innovative approach to adapting its performance and pay management techniques can be seen as part of an evolutionary approach to change. But it is also important to see change and innovation against the background of increasing competition in the telecommunications industry, in particular from the cable companies; BT's retaliation against reduction in market share through its 'win back' campaign and marketing of price reductions; fierce pressure on profit margins; and increasing labour market pressures and the consequent need for increased HR effectiveness.

Over the course of the last ten years, Mercury has shifted the emphasis from:

Individual performance	→	Individual contribution
Backward-looking	→	Perspective on the future
Responsibilities	→	Accountabilities
Line management ownership	→	Joint ownership by employees/line management
Standard market-led packages	→	Flexible market-led packages

The key goals for Mercury have been to empower line management; to strengthen the budgeting process; to train line management, and to communicate its approaches to people and pay management to all employees. The shift in approach to performance management has brought about fundamental change. The traditional approach to rating performance was disliked because employees were not sufficiently involved and 'part of' the process, the process link to pay was perceived as too strong, and the increasing diversity of working practices and patterns made a single approach inappropriate. Therefore, in the early 1990s Mercury developed its approach:

Annual review	→	Rolling reviews (where appropriate)
Increases corporately determined	→	Increases determined by managers
Annual review for all	→	Annual review where appropriate on basis of market, contribution, internal checks

The reward strategy has always been supported by a performance review system. The approach to performance management was overhauled in 1994 from a process that was:

- 'top down'
- ratings-driven
- lacking in choice
- lacking in employee ownership
- backward-looking
- annual

to one that is :

- jointly owned (by line managers and employees)
- based on the performance contract

- open to choice
- open to peer group involvement
- forward-looking
- skills-based.

A key element of the new approach has been to offer employees choice in how their contribution is reviewed. The table below highlights the selections made in 1994:

Choice of approach	%
Review of 1993–94 objectives	62
Performance contract	63
Accountabilities planner	64
360° feedback	25
Job-specific appraisal	19
Virtual team member review	14
Competence review	14
Blank sheet of paper	12

On the basis of this new approach, Mercury's management of pay has continued to emphasise the importance of salary budgeting as part of the financial planning process, managers informing their decisions with market data. Mercury has also developed techniques to provide internal checks and balances by providing detailed functional job analyses by location.

The development of the benefits strategy

The theme of choice within Mercury's contribution management system has been carried through to its approach to the benefits package, which commands an expenditure of over £50 million. The objective in increasing the element of choice was two-fold to make employees aware of the cost of benefits and to acknowledge that employees are not all the same, but have different needs and requirements. The 'flex' programme was piloted on 400 employees in

1994 – 34 per cent opted to vary their choices. In 1995 flex was made available to all employees and a similar percentage took advantage of this option. The elements of the package which can be 'flexed' are:

- pension
- life assurance
- healthcare
- annual leave
- dental care
- cars
- childcare vouchers

and all were designed to offer choice on a cost-neutral basis. In summary the choices are:

Pension
Accrual rate of 60ths and employee cost of 5 per cent can be traded for accelerated accrual rates of 55ths, 50ths, 45ths and 40ths. Contributions can be up to 15 per cent. In the pilot, one in ten employees opted for improved pension cover.

Life assurance
Four × salary life cover can be traded down to three × or two × salary in return for a cash credit.

Healthcare
All Mercury employees receive free healthcare on the basis of family status. 'Flex' allows employees to trade up or down.

Annual leave
The system enables employees to 'flex' up to five days' leave, allowing employees to trade down to 20 days or trade up to 30 days.

Dental care
A single-level dental care scheme was already part of Mercury's package. The 'flex' package provides an alternative, providing reimbursement for private treatment.

Cars
The company car policy already gave a 'cash in lieu' option. Mercury also introduced a lease-purchase scheme for employees to lease at their own cost.

Childcare vouchers
This offers a salary sacrifice option in exchange for childcare vouchers.

The flexibility programme has been promoted in a variety of ways – presentations, posters, company newsletters and 'flex packs' containing each employee's personalised choices. Independent financial counselling was supplied to help employees make their decisions through 'help line' services and 'surgeries'.

The spur for change came from Mercury's continuing drive towards a reward strategy geared to both corporate and individual needs. Flexible benefits were seen as the best way of containing benefits costs while getting maximum value for money.

All of these changes have been developed and introduced based upon clear business needs. They have therefore always been seen as line management tools rather than personnel-led programmes, and this has, to a large extent, been a major factor in their success.

FIRST DIRECT

> Midland Bank's decision to establish First Direct was very much driven by the need to meet changing customer demands. Operating in a 'green field', First

Direct needed to recruit, retain and motivate people with specific skills. This case-study examines the evolution of their pay philosophy and the link between career development, performance management and reward.

Background

First Direct is a division of the Midland Bank, which is in turn part of the Hong Kong and Shanghai Banking Corporation. It provides a 24-hour telephone banking service to personal customers and is based in Leeds.

First Direct started life in 1988 as a project named Project Raincloud. The brief of the project team was to develop an alternative delivery mechanism for personal banking customers.

Midland Bank took the decision to research this concept for two reasons. Firstly, there was a growing dissatisfaction, fuelled by the media, among the general public, with the perceived levels of service that banks were offering. The second reason was the opportunity that Midland saw, based on the 'purchasing habits' of its customers.

Midland had undertaken research in the late 1980s which indicated that one in five customers had not visited their branch in the last month and that one in ten had not been into the branch in the last six months. By choice, 51 per cent would prefer not to visit their branch at all and 34 per cent objected to having to make appointments. An astonishing 48 per cent had never had cause to meet their bank manager, and of those who had, 36 per cent said that it was more than one year ago.

On the basis of these facts, Midland took the bold decision to develop the concept of a high-quality telephone-based banking service and the Project Raincloud team was given 12 months to plan and launch First Direct.

The opportunities arising from the development of the

business as a 'green field' operation are numerous, but two in particular have been fundamental to First Direct's success. First, from an operational perspective, the business was built with the customer as the primary focus. The processes and systems that were developed for running the business looked at issues from the perspective of their impact on the customer.

In the banking environment this represented a fundamentally different approach. Traditionally, the development of such systems had been very much account-focused. For example, an individual with a mortgage account at one branch of Midland and a cheque account at another would be held in the system as two different customers. The First Direct system, however, provides a bank employee with all the available information about any particular customer at any particular time.

The second key benefit of setting up as a 'green field' site was the opportunity it presented to ensure that First Direct attracted what they considered to be the right people. Staff recruited into First Direct are selected not for their previous banking experience but on the basis of qualities, skills and attitudes that First Direct believes are necessary for providing a high-quality professional service to their customers.

Organisational culture

Since their launch in 1989 First Direct has nurtured and developed a very strong corporate culture, based on a clear set of organisational and personal values, and it has ensured that the culture and values that it aspires to internally are consistent with its external brand positioning, and hence the way it deals with its employees within the organisation is no different from the way that it deals with its customers.

The company philosophy holds that if employees enjoy coming to work, feel valued, and believe that their efforts and views count, then they will contribute more to the business in a variety of ways. First Direct believes that this additional employee contribution impacts on the bottom line – highly satisfied customers opt for more of its products and the resulting brand positioning, which is based on service and value, gives it a competitive advantage.

Business changes that led to the review

The First Direct reward and motivation strategy has evolved and become increasingly sophisticated since its launch in 1989. First Direct then employed 150 people, many of whom had been involved in the initial project team, and reward and motivation in this environment were relatively simple. The objective then was to ensure that people were being paid at an appropriate level while the rapid growth, the range and diversity of opportunities, and the success of the business took care of everything else.

By 1992 the position had changed significantly, with 600 people employed and an anticipated further trebling in size over the next two years. First Direct therefore began to address the issues of motivation and reward in a larger organisation. The company was keen to maintain the sense of being part of a small project team and to ensure that opportunities for development continued to be available to a substantial number of individuals.

However, in 1992 First Direct realised that it did not have the appropriate processes in place to facilitate the transition from a small project-based organisation to one employing over 2,000 people.

Within the first two years First Direct had concentrated

solely on getting the business up and running. Effort had focused upon developing the training and induction programmes, ensuring that the service quality ethic was supported from day one, and impressing the culture and values on everyone in the First Direct team. However, little work had been done on the processes required to support the management of these people's going forward; these were viewed as tomorrow's problems.

In 1992 it also became clear that the performance management and appraisal processes were regarded as being ineffective and unhelpful. The reward structure in place had been largely adapted from their parent, Midland Bank, and was not appropriate to the needs of the business. Furthermore, it offered little or no support for employees in terms of career development.

Developing an HR strategy

In 1992 First Direct developed an HR strategy designed to incorporate all of these key issues, and devised a plan to introduce a skills-based approach to recruitment, induction, performance management, career development and reward.

From an HR perspective, First Direct's overriding objective when developing the strategy was to ensure that it complemented the overall business objectives and that individuals at all levels within the organisation were involved in the development of its component parts. Above all, it was critical that this strategy was not seen as a personnel department initiative, but rather something which was owned by the company as a whole.

Having defined the overall strategy, the next step was to identify the core skills that were considered to be important to the business. Fifty employees from all levels within First Direct were involved in the process, which resulted in 12 core business skills being identified.

Using these 12 core skills as the basic building blocks, First Direct then involved a further 200 individuals in developing profiles for all roles within the organisation. The role profile serves a number of purposes: for each role it defines the skills and technical knowledge required, describes the broad tasks to be undertaken, and sets down the performance standards that will be required by individuals in that role.

The role profile provides the basis for a number of key management processes. For example, it describes the skills required for recruitment and development purposes; defines the performance standards needed for the performance management process, and provides the basis for the development of a skills-based pay structure.

By 1992 First Direct had identified the basic building-blocks and by 1993 had incorporated the role profiles into its new appraisal process, effectively introducing a skills-based approach to performance management. Having introduced the new appraisal process, First Direct conducted an employee opinion survey about the changes that had been made. The results showed that:

- 93 per cent of people felt positive about the changes to the process.
- 85 per cent felt that they were making a significant contribution to First Direct, and that this was generally recognised by the appraisal process.
- 68 per cent said that they felt that the exchange of views in the appraisal was valuable. While clearly there was plenty of room for improvement in this area, this result showed an improvement of almost 50 per cent over the previous system, where only 46 per cent of people felt the exchange was valuable.
- 75 per cent agreed with their final appraisal rating.

The new skills-based appraisal process has played a key role in the motivation of individuals within the business. Employees now have a much clearer idea of what is required of them in terms of skills and performance standards. They can see how they are performing against these standards and, ultimately, they can now have a far more structured discussion regarding areas for development.

Having introduced the new performance management process, in late 1993/early 1994, First Direct turned its attention to developing a skills-based approach to reward and career development.

The resultant 'drivers' for the remuneration changes

First Direct has changed its approach to reward quite significantly since its launch in 1989, when it simply adopted a version of Midland Bank's management pay and bonus policy. The Midland policy was based on a management-by-objectives process supported by performance-related pay and bonus. First Direct took the opportunity to apply these principles to all levels within the organisation, and under this process an individual was set objectives annually. At their appraisal individuals were given an overall rating based on their output, and this in turn determined both the level of base pay increase and the amount of bonus award. This process was operated within First Direct until 1993, when it decided to review this philosophy.

But why did First Direct feel the need to alter what many organisations would like to achieve – a truly performance-related pay and bonus structure? While First Direct absolutely supports the principle of differentiating reward based on individuals' achievement, there were large parts of the business where the structure that it had adopted initially was not appropriate, specifically in relation to performance-related pay.

A good example of this is First Direct's call centre, where there are groups of up to 600 individuals essentially undertaking the same role. Under the structure that was employed until 1993, if two individuals were each earning £10,000 per annum and in a particular year person A had a better year in performance terms than person B, then person A, in addition to a larger bonus, would have received a £500 salary increase compared with person B's £200 increase. If in future years they both performed identically, person A would still have gained year-on-year as a result of one good year. There were numerous areas within First Direct where similar scenarios would apply, and this prompted a fundamental review of how to structure reward packages in terms of base pay and bonus.

The approach that was adopted in 1993, while still supporting the concept of performance-related rewards, says that for two individuals doing the same role and requiring the same skills the base pay will be the same, and will be based on skills required and the appropriate market rate.

Differences in productivity between the two individuals are recognised and rewarded by differentiating their bonus payments, and are therefore performance-related.

The way the changes were developed and introduced

In summary, First Direct's current philosophy is that for base pay, salary increases will be based on market movements and on the basis of the skills required of an individual within a role. There is a rate for the job and base pay will not be directly performance-related. For bonus payments, the amount paid is based on the individual's level of performance and is productivity-related. The overall size of the pot available to spend is business-driven and will be related to the overall success of the business. As an example, in 1994 the business allocated 3.5 per cent to the bonus pot and payments ranged from 0 per cent to 12 per cent.

Having clearly established its reward philosophy, the final areas of the HR strategy that First Direct worked on during 1994 were the introduction of a career development framework and a supporting pay structure. Originally there was little or no help offered to employees in planning their career development. In addition, the pay structure, which was based on six very broad grades covering all levels within the organisation, was introducing barriers to progression as it did not recognise the range of skills that might be required within any one grade.

The new structure announced in September 1994 replaced the six grades with 10 development levels. Roles were assigned to a development level based on the range and complexity of skills required to undertake them. Despite increasing the number of development levels from six to 10, there were still the same number of reporting levels in the overall structure and therefore there was no increase to the reporting hierarchy.

The increase in development levels has simply recognised the differences in complexity of roles previously covered within the same grade and therefore paid at the same rate. First Direct hopes that this will provide it with the flexibility to offer greater scope for individual progression and development – critical in ensuring that its employees remain motivated and feel adequately rewarded.

As part of this new structure First Direct focused upon helping employees understand the possible career routes within the business. Roles have been clustered into 'job families' based on the skills required which take into account their overall purpose. For example, there is a 'people management family' which concerns managing through others, and a 'customer services family', where the key focus is the interface with customers. There are opportunities at a number of development levels within each job family and through this structure First Direct will be seeking to provide far more support to individuals facing career choices in the future.

In the short term First Direct aims to provide, as a minimum, a career guide outlining the different opportunities for development, and in the longer term to launch development centres where individuals can take time out to assess their strengths and preferences. Both of these initiatives will have the objective of helping individuals to decide which is the best development route for them based on their own individual skills and interests. The overall aim is to help employees make more informed career decisions.

First Direct believes that a clear and well-defined career development framework is an essential part of the motivation and reward equation. This is an area that will require much more work in 1996 and beyond. As an organisation First Direct believes in the need for continual change, and it realises that in order to keep ahead of its competition it will need to continue to harness the enthusiasm and potential of individuals within its business.

ROVER GROUP

> Rover faced intensifying overseas competition and suffered from an inheritance of industrial disputes and poor quality control. Turning the company round meant altogether changing the culture, in which the introduction of a single-status structure, performance management and pay, and people development policies played a major part.

Background

Rover Group Ltd is a wholly owned subsidiary of the German company, BMW.

Rover designs, manufactures and markets automotive products and operates with three sales marques: Rover, Land Rover and MG. Production exceeded 500,000 vehicles in 1995. 46 per cent of sales are to export markets and annual revenues are in excess of £5,000 million. Rover's workforce of 37,000 is based primarily in the UK in the Midlands (Birmingham), Cowley and Swindon.

In the late 1970s, British Leyland, the forerunner of Rover, had a history of inflexible working practices, industrial disputes, and products of questionable quality. It was facing the challenge of survival in the face of foreign competition, particularly from the Japanese. Its policy, steered by the then chairman, Michael Edwardes, was to consolidate the business and establish better management control over the company. At the same time a strategic link was made with Honda.

During the next few years the success of the Triumph Acclaim and the original Rover 200, both Honda-based cars, created a great willingness throughout the company to listen to new ideas and consider significant change.

In 1988 the company was acquired by British Aerospace. As a result, the company's priorities changed from dealing with Government departments to commercial performance with a focus on customer satisfaction. The new chairman, Graham Day, recognised that the company was ready to make the necessary dramatic improvements.

The board pursued two main priorities:

- satisfying external stakeholders, particularly customers and shareholders
- building a more participative management style to move forward with the workforce, based on a total quality management programme launched in 1987.

Also, by 1988 different union groups within the workforce had been integrated through a series of two-year pay deals linked to new working practices based on increased productivity, the introduction of new technology, and flexible working patterns. By then, Rover was already using best practice imported from Honda, including:

- statistical process control
- staff surveys and suggestion schemes
- a project-led approach to new models.

Organisation

Following streamlining of the former Austin Rover, Land Rover and Rover Group HQ structures into a single organisation in 1989, a project team of senior managers from manufacturing and engineering reviewed the company's processes, culture and management style. The outcome was a business organised as a single entity, focused around a central vision and mission with four main thrusts:

- growth of Rover's international business
- up-market focus for the company's products and image
- reducing the 'break-even' point
- delighting the customers.

To back up a revitalised product plan, major changes were made to company operations:

- manufacturing and engineering changed from functional organisational structures to highly autonomous and integrated business units
- new projects were driven by multi-functional teams instead of being split and driven functionally
- project managers were expected to stay with new projects for at least three years
- successful product outcomes took priority over functional target achievement

- the management structure was made much flatter with fewer grades within each level
- each operation identified critical success factors and strategic objectives as part of the ongoing planning process.

Company culture

Social and political changes, competitiveness in the motor industry and the special emphasis on environmental factors also created a requirement for a much broader business perspective to be adopted at all levels. In this setting, the resourcing of the company to ensure appropriate skills availability has become paramount, compensation being a key tool, as much in culture formation and development as in creating focus on achievement of key tasks, or as a targeted end-results incentive.

Rover's leadership style emphasises the company's high-level vision and strategic objectives and sets in place a good understanding of its core values and beliefs as well as clear objectives. The goal is to create a robust framework which, by constant communication, allows all individuals to understand the requirements of the business and their role and responsibility within it, without prescribing the method or specific process for delivering the objectives. A major focus of changed leadership style was the development of a distinctive Rover culture.

The association with Honda, the traditional BL site histories, and the previous management style have all influenced the development of different attitudes and different behaviours in recent years. The key changes have been to embrace this diversity, to recognise the talents of everyone in the company and aim to win a contribution from all associates.

Rover has used a programme entitled Total Quality Leadership to develop the original work on total quality of the late 1980s and to ensure that this remains lively and meaningful on a continuously developing basis. Rover has used its own self-assessment programme based on Baldridge, EFQM and British Quality Foundation type models, and indeed applied for, and was successful in winning, the UK Quality Award under the aegis of the British Quality Foundation. In such frameworks the various enablers are analysed in terms of effectiveness as well as more traditional measures of output and business results.

The organisation has changed in line with many over recent years, with a focus on project team organisation in matrix style. Some individuals hold more than one job title. Flatter structures, fewer levels, and minimal staffing in central roles providing either specialist inputs or strategic co-ordination have evolved. The norm is to devolve responsibilities, wherever sensible, to the lowest level with no job demarcations.

The organisation structures are now defined in terms of process requirement rather than vice versa. Rover's processes are analysed, designed and measured and subject to continuous review against best or better practice internally and externally. There is a saying in the business that everyone has two roles – doing the job and improving it – but for this to happen takes time, the necessary tools and techniques have to be learned.

Compensation strategy

In reward terms, the company has a history of moving from piecework, through measured day work, through very well targeted and structured productivity bonuses, into a situation where these were gradually consolidated into spot rates for each of five manual grades and salary bands for each of six salaried grades.

Against this background, therefore, the challenge was to

design, implement and maintain an appropriate compensation strategy to balance the following:

- individualism v team approach
- work groups v overall company performance
- control of current processes v innovation
- achievement of goals v calculated risk-taking
- individual contribution v market-related pay competitiveness.

The package also had to accommodate fundamental differences between the motivation of individuals and groups within the framework of a single-status organisation. This required a transparent, performance-based approach with differing elements to address differing recognition needs, the underpinning principle being to treat equally those who contribute equally. For Rover, single-status does not mean the slavish harmonisation of all terms and conditions but rather the removal of those differences which relate to status which cannot be justified by operational requirements or market competitiveness.

The compensation strategy follows the company's general people strategy, attempting to ensure that the business vision, the responsiveness to customers and the understanding of a general 'psychological contract' are taken into account. The strategy, therefore, focuses on individuals, reinforces line manager leadership, promotes development of the individual in both a business and personally-related way, and reinforces the importance of personal contribution. The compensation strategy agenda is determined by the management team. It is formulated taking account of business needs, the views and aspirations of associates and the reality of the prevailing collective bargaining environment (32,000 staff and manual associates are covered by the single-table bargaining structure).

While direct financial payments form a significant element of the compensation package, many other forms of reward are used, focusing on the individual. If differential performance leads to differential reward, then the reward structure must send messages that are consistent with stated beliefs and values.

The base salary approach for around 5,000 management and executive staff is completely merit-based. The pay planning process is separate from the performance and development review (PDR). The PDR emphasises individual performance against business and personal objectives, defines opportunities for personal development and skills requirements, and does not attempt to create an overall summary of performance which is then pay-related. A separate process exists for assessing payment using individual pay comparisons, perceived value of contribution and any market sensitivities.

Agreement was reached in November 1994 to consolidate the previous five hourly grades and six salaried grades into a single-status structure of just three levels. These will provide the opportunity to move away from spot rates to salary bands with higher pay for more responsibility. Introduction of the new integrated grading structure has been phased over two years to spread the cost of assimilation and give time for the introduction of the more efficient ways of working achievable with removal of the last remaining blue-/white-collar demarcations. Profit-related bonuses are also payable.

In the highest of the three classifications below management level (classification C), the approach is that of general awards plus merit. In the lower two grades a basic rate within a salary band is paid, eventually with the aim of making merit payments to all. A process of developing pay progression proposals for classifications A and B has met with some trade union resistance and further work is needed to secure full acceptance of the increased individualisation of reward. The challenge is to establish an individual review process which takes account of the manufacturing environment and its history of limited 'discretionary' contribution over and above the job requirements. The new process needs to be extremely robust as maintaining 'felt fair' consistency over such a large group will not be easy. It is imperative that the new arrangement is fully supported by line management if it is to deliver the strategic objectives of enhancing individual and team contribution. As the increasing body of research shows, an inappropriate performance-related pay scheme is ineffective at best, and at worst can degrade the critical relationship between the team leader and team members.

The focus on employment security, introduced as one element in the New Deal Agreement in 1992, has been perceived as a major benefit in which individuals feel freer to make improvement contributions which assist with the overall efficiency and effectiveness within the business. There is a constant striving to improve the work environment and to provide the necessary tools to do the job.

Rover has established better healthcare services and facilities and offers medical examinations to all associates on an annual basis or two-yearly basis depending on age. The emphasis on security and personal care creates a more positive environment in which to encourage greater contribution.

People development

To reinforce line management leadership Rover has established a much broader approach to upward and peer appraisal. This has been under way now for a period of three to four years, but is not used as a formal basis for linking financial reward.

Development opportunities are regarded as key to

individual satisfaction. In an environment with a much reduced hierarchy, the value of broader experience for ambitious individuals is increasingly regarded as positive. The transition from the traditional push for promotion to greater emphasis on personal development has occurred over the past two or three years. The demand now is for access to key projects and to have the opportunity to participate in interesting or challenging programmes where learning from Honda, working with BMW, associating with the key interfaces in the extended enterprise – ie dealers, distributors and suppliers – are roles that people press for.

The multi-functional project-based team approach also creates increased opportunities for leadership, thereby giving a greater sense of satisfaction for some individuals. For others the sense of personal responsibility on technical and professional issues is equally important.

As the company is growing internationally, overseas assignments are also more generally available. Learning programmes are increasingly externally accredited; a partnership degree is in operation with Warwick University, and an in-house MA in total quality leadership is accredited by Liverpool John Moores University. Rover also runs an extensive range of other programmes jointly with Warwick and Coventry Universities.

While the delayering of the organisation means that a much more sensitive approach to individual reward has to be taken because of the reduction in promotions and grade changes, the company finds that by being creative in making available other personal development opportunities employees' motivation can readily be sustained.

To promote focus on associate involvement, rewards through the suggestion scheme have been maintained. On an audited basis for 1994 the annual one-year savings from suggestions were valued at £8.5 million and payments of about £1.5 million were paid out. The suggestion scheme is in the process of being superseded by more flexible and team-based arrangements but it has been a major factor in encouraging employee contribution over the past seven or eight years.

More recently, corporate recognition events giving public credit to individuals and teams, and learning events where groups and individuals can share key learning points with colleagues across the company, have provided a focus on individuals who make special contributions. The development of a car lease scheme, not based on management status but on length of service, and pension scheme developments that give an opportunity to individuals to retire earlier than the normal retirement date as a flexible benefit have been well received.

Not all initiatives have been or will be successful. For example, in the late 1980s a bonus was introduced which linked payments to the quality rating given by customers after three months of car ownership. While the objective of securing real customer satisfaction data was laudable, the four to six months delay between building the car and getting the bonus undermined any motivational impact.

It is incumbent on the leaders of the organisation to take calculated risks and then monitor the effects on the 'motivational health' of the enterprise. Attitude surveys are a useful tool. In the 1994 viewpoint survey, 85 per cent of associates reported that they were very satisfied with Rover as a company to work for.

Rover's response to changing customer demands and the political and economic environment has emphasised the need to be flexible. The company must be competitive in order to maintain business and employment security. Given that the company strategy, culture, processes, and organisation are continuously changing then the compensation strategy will need to be equally flexible.

CHAPTER FIVE

The State of the Art in the Public Sector

Robert Elliott and Helen Murlis

There have been profound changes in the thinking behind public sector pay for most of the last decade. Much of that change imitates changes made over the last 15 years or so in the private sector. It has been driven both by the influence of broader international thinking on reforming the place and nature of the public service as a whole and, more specifically, by the beliefs and consequent policy initiatives of the Conservative Government which first took office in 1979. The UK reforms have rested on two principal ideas – competition and flexibility.

From the outset these policy initiatives emphasised market solutions and the importance of competition in the provision of both the inputs to and the outputs of the public sector. This competition has taken the form of market testing, the contracting out of some activities and the creation of quasi-markets both between and within public sector institutions. Contracting out has led to a reduction in the size of the public sector. Even where public sector employees have bid for and successfully retained the contract for provision of services, this has generally been accompanied by a sharp decline in the numbers employed.

More important as influences on public sector pay have

been the twin thrusts of performance-related pay and the progressive decentralisation of pay determination. This chapter focuses on these two influences and the way in which this policy is currently developing. It draws on experience from four public sector organisations at the forefront of these reforms:

- HM Customs & Excise – a large department taking an integrated approach to HR management and pay
- the Employment Service – a major Government agency among the first to take delegated responsibility for pay
- Derby City General Hospital Trust – an NHS Trust that has made major progress with local pay determination
- the Civil Aviation Authority – which has been independent for some time and has made a series of strategic moves in terms of rationalising and improving reward management within the organisation.

The pressures for reform

Macro-economic pressures
At the macro-economic level, pressures to contain public expenditure, of which public sector pay is the major component, grew as the UK entered the recession and the cyclical elements of the public sector deficit increased. More generally, the desire to reduce public expenditure reflected the now widespread acceptance by policy makers of the view that the public sector 'crowds out' private sector investment and expenditure and thus diminishes the size of the private sector. The defence of this view is the belief that the private sector drives wealth creation, a perception that ignores the public sector's critical role as the producer of both the human capital and the infrastructure essential to the growth process in an advanced economy.

Pressure to contain public expenditure may also conflict with the other goals set for public sector pay reform. Some reforms will require additional investment to implement effectively. If these macro-economic pressures have assumed less significance in the last two years, the impetus for reform has not abated and in central government has been driven by other factors. The most important of these has been the recent programme of fundamental expenditure reviews, often resulting in substantial cuts in overall running costs.

Heterogeneity of the public sector
The public service is far from homogeneous and the current programme of reform has sought to recognise this in structures and systems, including pay, which are fit for purpose. In central Government a distinction has been made between core activities, the policy making departments, and the peripheral activities, the agencies that administer the policy. Pay structures are being developed which are deemed more appropriate to the specific and often different labour market needs of each activity.

Lying behind these initiatives is the Citizen's Charter white paper (Cmnd 1559) of 1991 which outlined the principles and methods through which the Government sought to achieve better service delivery. It emphasised that the general drive to improve the performance of public sector employees might best be achieved by tying their pay to performance. The same philosophy is also reflected in the purchaser/provider split in the NHS and in the concurrent reforms in parts of local government.

Pay differentials and wage structure
Evidence suggests that in the past pay mechanisms have prevented the public sector from responding flexibly to changing labour market conditions. There has been an imbalance whereby manual workers in the public sector

earned more than their private sector counterparts, while senior grades in the public sector lagged further and further behind the private sector. One important consequence of this is a much more compressed public sector wage structure. The reform of public sector pay systems has been, and is being, designed in part to remove this imbalance.

Individualisation of pay – the performance factor

The drive to relate individual pay to performance started with more senior grades. The key milestones to date in this process have been:

- early 'test runs' among management grades in non-departmental public bodies, eg the Scottish Development Agency (1983)
- the experimental senior Civil Service bonus scheme which ran from 1985 to 1988 and was abandoned in favour of other policies
- initiatives at chief officer level and in some more junior grades in local government from the late 1980s – a few have since been abandoned
- a new scheme for the most senior grades of the home Civil Service, below Permanent Secretaries
- the individual performance review scheme for management grades at the top of the NHS
- a merit pay scheme for university staff, implemented in 1990
- cascading down of performance pay in the Civil Service to cover all white-collar grades through the early 1990s

Since the first moves in this area the approaches adopted have changed as the investment required to ensure that they operate in an acceptable way has been quantified. The focus now is increasingly on integrating pay policy with the performance planning cycle, emphasising personal development planning, looking at the 'how' as well as the 'what' of performance, often through competency-based approaches, and reinforcing the value of team contribution.

Competency-based approaches have taken two main forms. The first has focused on the skill sets required to deliver 'fully acceptable' performance, often by grade. For secretaries, for instance, this would include word processing, filing, making meeting and travel arrangements, and dealing with visitors. The second approach goes deeper, and looks at the key forms of behaviour associated with excellent performance. For a secretary, this might include planning and organising, initiative, assertiveness, concern for order, achievement and drive, each defined in detail in relation to behaviour that is identified as appropriate and successful within the organisation. Sometimes the two approaches are used together.

Employers are learning that it is much more important to raise the performance of employees rather than simply concentrate on the process of performance-rating and the distribution of the modest levels of reward available within a cash-constrained public sector. Attitude surveys confirm that most public employees accept the principle of differentiated reward. Their concerns now focus on the implementation of PRP, the fairness and consistency of both objective setting and assessments, the quality and constructiveness of feedback given, and the extent to which pay provides acceptable rewards to the fully acceptable performers.

The previous chapter illustrated that the new competency-based approaches in the private sector have resulted from the drive to improve employee training and development and to enable employees better to deliver their organisations' overall strategic goals. They may appear to be measuring inputs at the neglect of the quality of the output, the service delivered, but at their best they focus on outputs related to customer service standards and other measures equally relevant to public service performance. In many circumstances they are accepted by staff as having much greater value for the kind of work they are involved in, rather than purely results-based approaches. Derby City General Hospital Trust and HM Customs & Excise have both gone down this route.

After several years of continuous focus on performance improvement combined with stringent public sector expenditure controls, there are now some worries about the future for performance rewards. Employees express concern about the scope that exists for them to continue to improve their performance. The 'production process' in many public services appears to offer fewer opportunities than other areas to achieve manpower reductions without a deterioration in service. Without fundamental structural review and/or a redefinition of the workload it is hard to see how some parts of the public service can deliver much by way of performance improvements. Many employees, and it has to be said their unions, are beginning to see performance-related pay as a means of holding down paybill costs and as a real threat to the maintenance of the long-term purchasing power of their salaries which they became accustomed to under the service- and experience-based pay systems they have now largely left behind.

Decentralisation and pay delegation

The impetus for decentralisation of pay arrangements has grown in strength over the last five years. The rationale for devolution has come from a series of factors:

- the belief, based on observation of the practice in many

large private sector companies, that devolution produces a better strategic fit between reward and business strategy
- the view that the heterogeneity of most of the public service required a diversity of approach not possible under centrally-negotiated systems
- the desire to accommodate local and regional labour market pressures and cost variations, recognising that this is appropriate below the levels/specialisms where the recruitment market is, and always has been, national
- the perception that centralised performance-related pay arrangements are unlikely ever to work effectively because they tend to be seen as annual appraisal schemes based on centrally-designed systems and reporting procedures and related to a review cycle which is aligned to neither the values nor the operating cycles of individual organisations.

Discussion of these factors and of those initiatives that have emerged have had to contend with countervailing arguments which emphasise:

- the risk that pattern bargaining might emerge and of consequent pay leap-frogging leading to inflationary pay increases
- the constraints of a national market for clearly-defined roles in many specialisms
- the political convenience of some methods of pay determination, notably for those groups covered by pay review bodies (although this may now to be changing)
- the perceived inappropriateness of crude, individual, output-based performance-related pay systems for professional groups where qualitative measures and teamwork are dominant values.

Decentralisation has none the less been progressing across the whole of the public service in recent years. The key milestones over the last few years are:

- the break-up of the central Civil Service pay agreement into the constituent union bargaining groups and the associated move away from uniform annual settlements (a belated consequence of the implementation of some of the recommendations of the 1982 Megaw Report on Civil Service Pay)
- the development of the local government framework agreement which enabled individual local authorities to break away from national rates. This produced an initial flurry of breakaway arrangements which has largely petered out as a result of increasing cost controls and the requirement to implement new arrangements on a 'no detriment' basis because of reserved rights
- the establishment in successive waves of NHS Trusts which resulted initially in the devolution of pay arrangements for management grades and which is now extending slowly to clinical grades – with some encouragement from pay review bodies
- the creation of 'next steps' agencies in the Civil Service following the Ibbs Report which enabled large agencies to assume pay delegation, the first of which was HMSO in 1990
- the Government's decision, announced in the white paper 'The Civil Service – Continuity and Change' (Cmnd 2627, 1994) which required all departments and agencies to take full delegation for pay from 1 April 1996

A critical aspect of pay delegation has been that it has required agencies to develop and articulate strategic goals for their organisation. The assumption of responsibilities for pay and the management of human resources has required organisations to address the issue of the fit between their reward strategy and organisational goals. As a result they have now to consider their customers, the nature of the service they provide, and how best delivery of that service might be achieved in the 'business case' required by HM Treasury as part of the delegation process. This feature will be evident in some of the following case-studies.

That agencies have not come to address strategic issues as a consequence of assuming responsibility for pay is the reverse of the process that we observe in the private sector. As the previous chapter showed, the development of the human resource strategy should follow, not precede, the development of organisational strategy.

A second feature is evident from the following case-studies. Unlike the private sector, most of the organisations that have assumed responsibility for pay do not produce products or services which they sell to earn them revenue. The revenue they earn comes as a grant from the Exchequer. Unless this is adjusted in an appropriate manner the revenue they raise will fail to reflect the changing pattern of demand for their services. Moreover, the budget they receive may be reduced as a result of public expenditure controls or a fundamental expenditure review. The revenue available to reward and develop human resources is, therefore, to some degree outside the control of the agency and this requires a different approach to reward strategy.

THE CIVIL AVIATION AUTHORITY

> The first study reports the experience of the Civil Aviation Authority Agency which was among the first to break the links with the Civil Service pay structure, and which has now, through a series of stages, delegated control over pay within the organisation.

Introduction

The CAA has three basic functions. The Economic Regulation Group (ERG) regulates airport charges and advises on air transport policy. The Safety Regulation Group (SRG) regulates the industry by ensuring that aircraft and airport standards are set and maintained, and that key staff in the industry are regularly checked and licensed. The largest group is National Air Transport Services (NATS) which provides air traffic services across Britain and at many of the UK airports including Heathrow, Gatwick, Manchester and the Scottish lowlands.

In total the CAA employs some 6,500 staff, 2,500 of whom are shift workers in NATS. NATS in total employs some 5,300 staff, SRG having 800 and ERG and the Corporate Group 400. Other than in NATS, shift working does not occur significantly. Whereas NATS in its operational areas tends to train its own staff in basic skills, eg air traffic controllers and maintenance engineers, other parts of the CAA, particularly SRG, need to recruit from the appropriate industries, for example pilots and aircraft maintenance engineers. The CAA's workforce is generally professional and technically biased, covering a wide range of disciplines.

The CAA workforce is highly unionised, with particular concentrations of union members in the operational areas. Among air traffic controllers and their assistants and maintenance engineers membership is close to 90 per cent and it is over 80 per cent among the pilots. Union membership has steadily declined among administrative, clerical and managerial staff, where it now averages some 30 per cent. Unions are, however, recognised for collective bargaining purposes for all groups of employees, with the exception of those on personal contracts who number some 250.

The main union recognised by the CAA is the Institution of Professionals, Managers and Specialists (IPMS) which represents, among others, air traffic controllers, maintenance engineers and pilots. They have some 2,200 members within the CAA. The Clerical and Public Services Association (CPSA) has some 1,400 members within the CAA, representing air traffic control assistants as well as clerical and secretarial staff. The National Union of Civil and Public Servants (NUCPS) covers administrative and some managerial disciplines, and the Manufacturing, Science and Finance Union (MSF) represents the craft and general unions. NUCPS and the craft and general unions have few members in the CAA, especially compared with IPMS and CPSA who lead on the major negotiating issues.

From its formation in 1972 the CAA developed its own terms and conditions with the exception that its pay and related allowances, such as London weighting, reflected Civil Service rates and structures. As time passed, the practice of determining part of the employment package in house, with part being determined by Civil Service settlements, became increasingly inappropriate to the CAA's circumstances, and the pay round did not provide opportunity to pursue management objectives. During 1986 and 1987 the various groups of staff according to union representation were negotiated out of the Civil Service arrangements.

The break with the Civil Service

The inappropriateness of Civil Service terms to the CAA became of increasing concern to CAA management as they sought to implement changes in organisational structures and working practices and arrangements. Management realised that to achieve significant change they needed to control all terms and conditions and to relate compensation to the needs of the business, especially as severe recruitment and retention problems had developed in some key areas where staff had a high market value. It was also appreciated that in order to develop and empower managers the CAA had to assume control over all its terms and conditions.

The breaking of the Civil Service links was both costly and messy. The negotiations were protracted because the new arrangements for each functional group were negotiated separately, and staff generally had to be satisfied that the change was in their interests, both long and short term. The changeover was expensive because the unions required the relativities to be preserved between one group and another, and an adherence to the 'pay spine' where each step was worth 4 per cent.

The internal inheritance was not favourable to management's cost control. During the period when Civil Service arrangements applied, a considerable number of allowances had been introduced in order to achieve flexibility and change. Over the years many of these allowances had become, in effect, unnecessary, but they continued because there was no direct control over the annual settlement level. This was because of the inability to abandon them as part of the annual pay round and partially because of the pay spine which made any absorption into basic pay disproportionately expensive. By the late 1980s allowances numbered nearly 100.

The initial management approach

What was clear during the 1989 pay negotiations was that management did not have sufficient information and computer support properly to cost every element of the paybill. This was remedied for the 1990 and subsequent negotiations. The amounts spent on every allowance, the numbers who received each allowance, their level, and where they were based, was logged into the pay model, as was the percentage of the paybill used for each allowance. It was then very easy to cost any potential change in any element of pay. The system had also been developed to track trends in allowances over the previous year.

Benefits were also broadly costed; for example, the percentage worth of a day's annual leave and the proportionate worth of leave allowances. Similarly, the percentage worth of average sick absence was costed.

Managers were alerted to the costs of employing people at every level and were also made aware of the costs of filling jobs, particularly on a shift basis. In preparation for the 1990 and 1991 pay rounds there were significant consultations with selected managers to establish the terms and conditions that they regarded as unhelpful and where they would like changes. Particular attention was given to allowances, to establish those that were redundant. Discussions also centred on how pay resources were used. The most significant points to emerge from this period of consultation were that the compensation package was far too complex for most people to understand how their pay was calculated, and therefore there was no clear link between pay and performance. Other points to emerge were that the then performance-related pay arrangements, inherited from the Civil Service, were expensive and not motivating, and that the levels of shift compensation were a bar to achieving flexibility of movement between shift and day working. There was also a general appreciation that the pay spine was inflexible and expensive to maintain.

The development of the 1990 pay strategy

The 1990 pay round was unexceptional except that it covered all changes that would occur to pay and benefits during the year, but management were gaining more control over the total paybill and the monitoring process was providing information that covered a full twelve-month period. However, during 1990 the management approach was being developed which, in a paper to the CAA's executive committee that autumn, was described as a 'framework for implementation over the next three to five years'.

A series of executive papers during the autumn of 1990 and the spring of 1991 developed from some simple aims of pay and benefits to a comprehensive strategy for achieving those aims. The adoption of these papers ensured top management commitment to the aims, and a consistent and united management approach to their achievement over the following years.

The agreed management aims of the compensation systems were straightforward. They were to:

- support corporate objectives
- ensure the CAA could recruit, retain and motivate high-calibre staff
- develop closer relationships between pay and individual performance
- move towards individual pay's being mainly determined by line managers
- provide simple and flexible pay structures.

To achieve these aims it was also agreed that management would:

- retain median/upper quartile market pay position
- recognise that pay should reflect fragmenting markets in terms of particular skills/competencies, regions and levels
- reflect the 'managers must manage' culture that the CAA was developing.

The strategy also clarified what management viewed as the respective roles of management and the unions. These were that unions would negotiate rates of pay and conditions for specific groups, but managers took decisions on individual pay movement or lump sum awards. It was also agreed that managers' budgets would reflect their ability to exercise their prerogatives

Implementation of the strategy

As part of the preparation for the 1991 pay round, management provided a 'position paper' which, in addition to pay-market information, also set out the broad management aims in the forthcoming negotiations. This meant that, in general terms, the unions were aware of the management approach and that a policy of 'no surprises' was being implemented.

Management did, however, surprise the unions by declaring its detailed objectives in its opening proposals for the 1991 settlement level. This pre-empted the unions' claim and effectively set the agenda for the negotiations. The management initiative included a two-year deal which substantially increased basic pay. However, it also required the abandonment of many outmoded allowances, complete reform of the performance pay system, and revision of some aspects of terms and conditions. For the first time in the CAA's history the unions were faced with having to make concessions to achieve a settlement. After some six months of negotiations a settlement was reached which set management firmly on the path of the reform of the pay structures and allowances.

The costing of the 1990 and 1991 to 1993 settlements proved very accurate. The 1991 settlement was followed by the negotiation of a new performance pay scheme which was separate from the appraisal system and which was budget-driven to a significant extent, with managers taking decisions about awards. It has not yet proved possible to extend the performance pay scheme to the engineering areas, primarily because of Government pay policy which did not allow for the proposed pay structures for these staff.

The management of the CAA also took a decision not to develop performance pay systems for operational staff, such as air traffic controllers and their assistants, as they are expected to perform their duties fully and well at all times and within the systems and procedures set down. Any initiatives that are outside the set procedures could possibly impair the safety of operational systems, and it was therefore decided that initiatives in this area must not be encouraged by reward systems.

Currently some 2,500 of the CAA's staff are subject to performance pay but, when the opportunity permits, it will extend the system to encompass some 4,000 of its 6,500 staff.

The 1991 deal also resulted in the disappearance of the pay spine because the deals involving, in some instances, the abolition of allowances in exchange for increases in basic rates broke the pay spine, and functional groups now have their own pay structures.

Changes in the bargaining arrangements

In the Autumn of 1992 the unions were informed that the 1993 negotiations would be the last centralised settlement. The unions opposed this during the first part of 1993, but eventually entered into negotiations on new arrangements which led to eight bargaining units to settle pay and related allowances, but allowed for matters such as annual leave allowances, maternity and sick pay and pension benefits to be determined on an across-the-board basis.

The unions were convinced that they should agree to the devolution of pay bargaining in the light of a continuance of the 'position paper' preceding the annual pay round. This paper includes the philosophies set down by the executive, and provides a framework for the negotiators.

Government policy on pay

The Government limitation on pay increases for 1993, and the setting of criteria for settlements, proved a mixed blessing. Certainly it reduced the initiatives that managements might have taken to develop pay and related structures in recent years. It also centralised decisions on what could be afforded by organisations in the public sector, and will have inhibited flexibility in devolution over the next few years. On the other hand, it provided a breathing space within which managers could develop their negotiating skills without creating very difficult industrial relations situations. The new negotiating arrangements proved successful during the 1994 pay round with a variety of settlements but all within the financial and other parameters set down, occasioned to some extent by Government pay policy.

The way ahead

Pay philosophy and approaches need to be constantly reviewed to ensure that they relate to the needs of the organisation and support management initiatives. The economic and fiscal climate are also relevant to pay markets. What has become abundantly clear is that comparatively low inflation, coupled with the Government's public sector pay policy is highlighting that current pay structures in the CAA are not yet developed to the point where they are fully appropriate to current circumstances. Incremental steps in operational areas and standard performance pay progressions are equivalent to 4 per cent of the maximum of the scales. At a time when inflation was relatively high, this level of standard movement was acceptable. When such progression increases the paybill by 2 per cent – the same cost as the 1994 annual settlements – and paybills have to remain constant, then this level of increase, which is outside management control, becomes unacceptable. Planning within the CAA is directed at bringing in pay structures and arrangements which bring individual pay movements fully within management control, and therefore allow for adjustment according to the circumstances. The Authority also has a policy of devolving control over pay levels and movements as far as is practicable down the management chain.

Conclusion

The evolution of pay and benefits structures, levels and arrangements continues as the requirements of management change. By keeping the purposes of pay and benefits constantly under review, personnel managers can add value to their organisation. The CAA management would not pretend that it has not made mistakes in its approaches to pay and benefits over the past five years, or that the present arrangements are entirely satisfactory. However, the present arrangements are much closer to the management needs than they were five years ago, and the continual setting of aims and objectives within a consistent framework should enable progress to be maintained.

THE EMPLOYMENT SERVICE AGENCY

> The Employment Service assumed agency status four years ago and employs a workforce which is deployed throughout the UK. The opportunity to employ a regional or local approach to pay clearly

exists, but has been deemed inappropriate in this case. Yet there were important changes in the reward structure that the assumption of responsibility for pay has enabled the agency to make, and it took the opportunity to review how appropriate that structure was to its organisational needs. The human resource strategy is still in the process of development, and alignment of this with the strategic goals of the organisation is emerging.

The Employment Service

The Employment Service (ES) is an executive agency within the Department for Education and Employment. The ES exists to help carry out Government employment policies, and particularly to promote a competitive and efficient labour market which encourages the growth of employment and the reduction of unemployment. Performance targets agreed with the Secretary of State as part of the annual performance agreement (APA) include total numbers of unemployed placings achieved (numbers helped back into work). The ES works through a comprehensive network of Employment Service Jobcentres (ESJs), and currently has some 51,500 staff, of which 67 per cent are in the clerical grades, 32 per cent in middle management grades, 0.5 per cent specialist posts, and 0.5 per cent in senior management grades.

ES pay strategy

The aim of developing specific ES pay and grading arrangements is to put in place structures which deliver value for money, and which support the delivery of ES business targets.

In order to deliver its APA targets, the ES needs to encourage its best managers to work in the field, managing local offices. The Civil Service grading structure did not differentiate, in pay terms, between the demands of particular posts, ie between policy and delivery jobs, or between more demanding field posts (large, inner-city offices) and less demanding field posts (small rural offices). This led to a situation in which there was no incentive for managers to remain in field posts as there was no pay lead for local office manager posts, and the perceived wisdom was that promotion opportunities were more plentiful in the regional and head office policy and support structures. Additionally, it was proving difficult to attract field managers to manage large inner-city offices, since they could earn as much for a less demanding post elsewhere. This often led to the inner-city offices' being managed by less experienced managers, and in some cases by promotees.

There was also a desire to overhaul performance appraisal systems, so that performance could be assessed against individual performance objectives which were measurable and which relate directly to ES business objectives.

Pay and grading developments in the ES are seen as one element in the development of performance management arrangements. The role of pay is therefore seen as supporting:

- vacancy filling, by signalling the value of the job to the organisation and attracting people with the competencies needed
- performance appraisal, by rewarding people for meeting and exceeding the required standards and objectives
- individuals in developing and applying the experience and expertise they need to improve their performance.

A staged approach

Grades 4 to 7
The first stage was to job evaluate all grade 4 to 7 posts, using the Treasury system, 'Job Evaluation and Grading Support' (JEGS). JEGS replaces the previous system, Quantified Factor Analysis (QFA), and was developed by the Treasury to take account of the greater importance attached to management of people and resources implicit in the setting up of executive agencies. A rank order of posts using QFA would place policy posts at the top of the list, whereas a rank order of posts using JEGS would place field management posts at the top. The use of JEGS was therefore consistent with the ES strategic aims.

The evaluation of grade 4 to 7 posts was used to differentiate between posts in job weight terms. Basic pay was still determined by the grade of the post and the individual, but performance pay awards were based on an equity share system. This means that the available performance pay budget can be fixed by the ES, in negotiations with the unions, and the budget is then divided up into shares for individuals which are determined by the job weight of the post (ie the SMPB to which the post is allocated) and individual performance. Performance appraisal marks are decided by line managers using a new four-box mark performance agreement, aligned to the business year. These arrangements were introduced from April 1993.

Executive officer posts (SEO, HEO and EO grades)

The second stage was to evaluate all SEO, HEO and EO posts and to allocate them to one of seven management pay bands (MPBs). The number of pay bands was determined by analysing the results of a benchmark evaluation of a sample of ES posts and identifying the number of discrete groupings of posts, relative to the job evaluation scores, which were present.

Both basic pay and performance pay are determined by the MPB to which the post has been allocated. Similar performance appraisal arrangements have been introduced for these posts and vacancy filling is competency-based, with all posts in the structure open to all individuals, whatever MPB their current post has been allocated to. These arrangements were introduced from April 1994, with assimilation arrangements for all staff in the previous grades.

The new structure provides more flexibility to design posts to meet specific business needs and to attach a higher level of pay to posts that fall at the top end of the job weight range for the previous grade. The MPB grading structure is increasingly being used by managers to delayer management structures. Over time, and given projected levels of turnover, the new structure will also enable the ES to demonstrate greater value for money from the paybill.

Inevitably, assimilation arrangements have proved difficult to manage in that it was necessary to implement the new structures without the need for up-front investment. The commitment that has been given is that the pay of the existing grades would be maintained, as at 1 April 1994, which means that the agency will not incur additional costs, but it does also mean that it will not necessarily be possible to increase the pay ranges for the assimilation pay bands without increasing costs overall. Despite this limited 'no detriment' policy, there has been a significant dip in the morale of staff in posts that have been allocated to the lower pay bands for each grade, given that they have an expectation that pay ranges will rise on an annual basis. There is also a feeling on their part that they were just unlucky to be in those posts on 1 April 1994 which have been allocated to lower pay bands. Movement from assimilation pay bands to MPBs is on a voluntary basis and incentives have been offered in the form of annual settlements that increase the maximums available on MPBs.

Clerical grades
A review of clerical, support, typist and secretarial grades has also taken place, and similar arrangements for these grades have been introduced from April 1995. For these grades the range of job weight is more restricted and the priority was to bring the clerical, support, typist and secretarial grades into a single pay band structure, rather than to differentiate between the high- and low-weight posts in the existing grades.

Changes are also necessary in order to bring the paybill for these grades, which form the vast majority of ES staff, under the agency's control. Under the national core agreement, pay awards consisted of steps up a pay spine, the number of steps determined by a performance box mark. Under the equity performance pay system, the ES will be in a position to set the overall value of the available performance pay budget and then to allocate shares on the basis of individual performance box marks. Whereas previously the cost of pay awards may have required reductions in overall staff numbers, the ES will have more flexibility to reduce the value of performance pay awards and/or reduce overall staff numbers.

Grades 6 and 7
In addition, from April 1995, senior management grades 6 and 7 were assimilated into the pay band structure – a single pay band covering grade 6 posts and two pay bands covering grade 7 posts. This change anticipated the creation of the Senior Civil Service structure, covering grades 5 and above, and completed a 12 pay band structure covering all Employment Service posts below the Civil Service-wide Senior Civil Service.

Industrial relations

It has been necessary to create new bargaining groups in order to negotiate these changes, and the interface issues that are being identified as the agency seeks to bring the structures together mean that further changes may be required. Formal agreements of short-term duration have been reached with the various unions, which codify their rights of access to information, etc.

The management team was kept at practitioner level (pay division and industrial relations team), all of whom had received negotiation skills training. The ability of the unions to negotiate is improving and the long lead up to the implementation of new grading structures helps to establish constructive working relationships. This is a new process for the lay officials involved (and for many of the full-time officials).

1995 saw a sustained campaign of selective industrial action on the part of CPSA, the largest clerical civil service union, in opposition to an imposed pay settlement. The action was unsuccessful and, in marked contrast, the union recommended acceptance of the 1996 pay offer.

In order to inform a strategy for annual negotiations, the ES commissioned a study by Hay Management Consultants of comparable rates of pay for ES posts. The data will assist in setting levels of recruitment and retention allowances (RRA) when looked at together with available data on levels of recruitment and wastage. It will also enable management to position the ES in the market place, in terms of the rates of pay offered elsewhere. It is not expected that the ES will move away from national pay settlements and rates of pay in the short term. However, the Service will use the Hay data to establish whether regionally-based settlements are a viable option for the future.

Job evaluation

The ES has trained a significant number of people in the use of the JEGS job evaluation system, in order to carry out benchmark exercises, to implement the new arrangements, and to provide support to line managers who are restructuring. It has made the process as transparent as possible and has used the results of the benchmark exercises to produce detailed banding guidance, which replaces the existing grading guidance. The banding guidance is freely available to line managers and can be used by them to design posts and to estimate the cost implications of changes.

Communications

The ES has used a variety of means, including presentations, newsletters and videos, to communicate plans, work in progress and decisions on pay and grading changes. It has evaluated its communications and found that no single medium suits the entire audience.

The ES has formally decided to communicate little and often, through line managers' briefings, leaving it to them to decide how information is further disseminated. Briefings are supplemented by summary newsletters giving the headlines and referring staff to their line managers if they wish to know more. The objective of this approach is to give line managers ownership of the changes and provide a feedback loop to those working on pay, appraisal and vacancy-filling development.

In addition, a major review of the pay strategy was carried out in the early part of 1996 and feedback was thereafter sought from staff through targeted questionnaires and a general invitation to write in with their views.

Realising the benefits of the new structures

Making radical changes to Civil Service pay and grading arrangements is a process fraught with difficulties and it is essential to have a clear view of what the business priorities are. Even with very clear strategic objectives, the process of change is a demanding one, embracing as it does the means by which people are appraised, how jobs are filled, and how people are rewarded. People who are affected bring many preconceptions to bear, not least the experience of others in implementing performance pay arrangements. The use of the term 'performance pay' is misleading, since the ES arrangements detail how the available budget is shared out in an equitable way rather than correspond to a performance-driven pay system as it is generally understood.

The funding of agencies and departments does not allow for any direct link between the money available to fund pay awards and the level of performance achieved by an agency. In the ES, given the nature of performance targets, there will always be a close link between the achievement (or otherwise) of those targets and the performance of the economy as a whole. Individual effort does play an important part but ultimately may not be the critical factor affecting overall results.

However, by breaking up the Civil Service grades into pay bands that have a more limited pay range, the ES is able to pay more for more demanding jobs, and less for less demanding jobs. Paybill drift will be arrested, in that people will be held at the maximum for the pay band, with performance pay paid as unconsolidated awards, unless they are willing (and able) to take on more demanding posts within a higher pay band. This gives line managers a significant degree of flexibility to reward people through basic pay. The use of an equity share system for performance pay awards ensures that the available budget for performance pay can be controlled and can be directed to the good performers.

Increasingly, line managers are becoming aware of the possibilities that the new structures provide to deliver their targets more effectively and, potentially, at lower cost. Managing the paybill in this way has not to date been a prime concern for line managers – staff costs have been largely taken for granted. Top management will clearly need to consider how far accountability for paybill costs can be delegated down the management line. Whether the new structures are successful in the aims set for them will ultimately depend on the use made of them by line managers. If posts are to be attractive to people of the calibre that they need to deliver their targets, they will need to be clear at what level decisions can be made and whether there is added value in the management layers they currently have, or plan to have.

Experience to date of applying the new structures in situations where there are opportunities to delayer suggests that they provide a more flexible framework with which to design robust posts with appropriate rates of pay that match the levels of responsibility required. There is, in addition, a measurable reduction in overall costs.

A review of progress

The Employment Service is currently reviewing the changes that have been made, in order to evaluate their continuing fit with business needs. Feedback has been sought from staff and line managers. Consideration is also being given to the impact of the transfer of benefit payment functions to the Benefits Agency on the introduction of the Job Seekers' Allowance, from October 1996. This change will lead to a major shift in the design of front-line delivery posts, accompanied by a significant investment in IT which will require a more multiskilled, flexible workforce. This in turn may require a more flexible approach to the grading of posts and a greater use of broad pay bands.

DERBY CITY GENERAL HOSPITAL

Few hospitals have developed comprehensive pay structures that fit their needs since the assumption of Trust status. Derby City General Hospital is one of those. The minimum conditions of a majority of employees in all Trusts, nurses and doctors, are still established by pay review bodies. Yet it is clear that these national rates may not be appropriate to local needs in some (or all?) cases and that an integrated reward strategy is required. One feature of this study is that substantial changes in grading structures may involve substantial transitional assimilation costs. Where organisations have to absorb these in first-year running costs, this may leave no resources to achieve other important changes.

Organisational background

Derby City General Hospital became a Trust in April 1993 as part of the 'third wave'. The Trust employs some 2,000 staff, most of whom are based at the 471-bed Derby City General Hospital, with a smaller number based at a second hospital, the 77-bed Derbyshire Children's Hospital. About half of the Trust's employees are nurses, midwives or healthcare support workers. The level of unionisation is around 50 per cent of the workforce, the Royal College of Nurses (RCN), the Royal College of Midwives (RCM) and UNISON being the three main unions.

Business changes that led to the review

With the advent of Trust status for Derby City General Hospital, the Trust was keen to develop new pay and grading arrangements which reflected and supported its intention to meet the challenges of the future.

Prior to the programme of NHS reforms, pay and grading arrangements were dealt with nationally under the Whitley framework. As a consequence, individual provider units such as Derby City General had little or no freedom to develop pay and grading arrangements which reflected and supported their local needs and objectives. While the NHS reforms allowed this to happen, in themselves they do not explain why it was essential for the Trust to develop its own local arrangements.

Motivation for these developments

In common with most healthcare organisations, Derby City General is under continuing pressure to deliver higher volumes and quality of services for less cost. Demand for healthcare services continues to grow exponentially, while the ability of most governments in developed countries to fund services declines.

With the assistance of external consultants, the Trust decided to begin by reviewing pay and grading arrangements for nurses and midwives. There were two reasons for this choice:

- Pay costs represent 75 per cent of total costs in the Trust, nurses and midwives together representing approximately 50 per cent of this.
- Nurses and midwives represent two of the most critical groups of employees, in terms of their impact on the quality of patient care.

The main advantages of local pay determination for the Trust were seen as the ability to develop a more flexible grading structure, tailored to local needs, and to reward good practice by linking pay to the measurement of individual employees' professional contribution. The Trust was also concerned that the new pay arrangements should set the tone for the future, in creating a much stronger link between pay and performance than had been the case under Whitley pay arrangements.

Critical elements in change

The first critical requirement was for the Trust to be clear about what it was trying to achieve. In this context, the following objectives were agreed:

- to improve the quality of patient care
- to reduce the costs of care by increasing labour efficiency and flexibility
- to improve job satisfaction by providing challenging career development opportunities for individual job holders.

In order to make this happen a number of critical elements needed to be in place:

Clarity of strategic direction
The Trust board has clearly articulated an overall human resource strategy linked to the business plan. This provided the context within which the project was designed and managed.

Top level commitment and drive
The project was characterised by an outstanding level of commitment and personal involvement from executive

directors of the Trust, including the chief executive, the director of nursing, and the director of human resources.

Line management leadership
Both the director of nursing and the head of midwifery provided significant and visible leadership. This was critical in order to establish and maintain credibility with professionals and ensure that it was not perceived as a 'personnel initiative'.

Extensive staff participation in research and development
The extent of direct staff participation in the project was a key element of success, and its significance cannot be overestimated. In total over 20 per cent of the nursing and midwifery workforce took part in the research, which involved the identification by a number of focus groups of the distinctive contributions of nurses and midwives, and the completion of an extensive questionnaire to identify individual job roles.

The focus groups discussed how good performers differed from poor performers, and how the issue of rewards should be approached. There was a large degree of consensus as to the key qualities of nurses and midwives who performed their jobs well. These were identified as attributes such as adaptability, kindness, reliability and resilience. The focus groups also concluded that a reward system should be able to differentiate between good and poor performers.

Simultaneously the questionnaire was distributed to a wider layer of staff who had volunteered to complete the document. About 80 nurses completed the questionnaire, giving details of the content of their job, and their attitudes to reward issues.

The management had approached the project with the hypothesis that the existing nine-grade clinical grading structure did not fit very well with the actual job roles performed by nurses. The conclusions reached by the focus groups and the results of the questionnaires bore this out.

Making the performance/pay link
The NHS, as with other public sector employers, is under considerable Government pressure to use PRP to develop a more 'performance-orientated culture'. Making the link between pay and performance has enabled the trust to drive a cultural change from time-served to performance-linked movement through a pay spine. By designing a scheme which rewards the qualities and behaviours of nursing and midwifery staff, the Trust believes it has also been able to improve the quality of patient care.

Leading-edge technology
The success of the project was built upon a sound technological base. With assistance from external consultants the Trust developed a competency model which was used as the basis for defining individual roles and the characteristics of high performers. Use of this technology, combined with extensive staff participation, ensured a high degree of credibility and reliability for the subsequent development of a new pay and grade structure.

The way the changes were developed and introduced

One of the main outcomes of the research was the identification of five distinct jobs roles performed by nursing and support staff. The new pay structure was framed around these. Compared with Whitley, the new structure is flatter and less hierarchical, with longer grade ranges, each replacing more than one existing grade. One of the other key features of the new structure is the ending of automatic service-based incremental progression. The rate at which individuals progress through their grade will be determined by an annual assessment of their individual contribution against clinical, behavioural and qualitative standards.

An intensive period of negotiations over the pay structure took place early in 1994. For the purposes of the negotiations, a staff-side committee was established with local and full-time representatives from the RCN, RCM and UNISON. Since then the Trust has concluded a recognition agreement with about a dozen trade unions. The negotiations centred around the details of the reward package and the assimilation arrangements. However, the management made it clear that the guiding principles of the new pay structure, which came out of the research project, were non-negotiable.

Overall, the new package has meant a very slight initial increase in the total nursing paybill, in part due to the costs of assimilation. However, the Trust believes that the advantages of the new system, in particular the scope for greater flexibility, and the move away from automatic increments to increments dependent upon levels of performance, justify the cost.

By the end of April 1994, 261 nurses previously on Whitley terms had opted to sign the contracts. Along with the nurses already on Trust contracts, this meant that over 60 per cent of the nursing workforce are now on the new terms and conditions.

Lessons learned

Whilst the Trust believes that the project has been a major success to date, there is equally a realisation that the process is a continuing one. Some of the key issues that need to be addressed for the future are the following:

- One of the outcomes of the project has been that the Trust has begun to recognise the significance of managerial

style, for example that of ward managers and ward sisters, as a determinant of individual performance. Consequently, if the new pay and grade arrangements are to achieve their potential, the issue of the individual managerial style of key individuals needs to be addressed.
- The Trust recognises that the organisational culture needs to support the new roles, and the expectations of the individuals in them, if their full potential is to be achieved. If the overall culture of the organisation does not reflect and support new imperatives, then there is a risk that the work that has been done to develop new roles and pay and grading arrangements will be neutralised by an inappropriate culture.
- There is no doubt that the project has been innovative and successful, largely because the Trust didn't 'put the cart before the horse' by developing new pay arrangements before rethinking some fundamental questions, such as what roles they wanted to be performed in the future. However, the Trust recognises that potentially there is a huge area to be explore beyond this, at the level of the design of patient care processes. If, because of cost or quality pressures, the Trust decides to take this step with other staff groups, there is little doubt that it will again need to rethink the nature and type of the jobs that are performed in the organisation, and the most appropriate pay and grading arrangements to support this.

HM CUSTOMS & EXCISE

> The final case-study reports the experience of an organisation with clearly stated and widely understood organisational goals, HM Customs & Excise. How to meet these goals has been the focus of the reforms within the agency. The emphasis has been on linking pay to performance, but pay ranges have been retained and it is progress up the range which is linked to performance.

Organisation background/employee environment

HM Customs & Excise is managed by a board of commissioners, which has a statutory responsibility for the collection of customs and excise duties, VAT, and for the enforcement of import and export prohibitions and restrictions.

The operational work of Customs & Excise and the provision of major services (eg solicitor's office, information technology) is organised into 'next steps executive units'. Headquarters offices are located in London, Southend, Liverpool and Manchester. Direction and accountability for the work of the department is achieved by linking three levels of planning – departmental, executive unit, and operational unit, and by a system of published annual reports.

The department employs about 26,000 staff and has a total annual budget of approximately £900m. The revenue collected represents around 45 per cent of the total yield from central Government taxation and totalled £66.6bn in 1993–94. In the same year a total of 8,510 drug seizures were made with an estimated street value of £1,980m. Over 4,000 offenders were dealt with by way of prosecution or fines in compounded settlements.

Strategic issues

Like many organisations in the public sector, Customs & Excise has had to take account of a range of external factors in setting operational and management priorities. In particular:

- the Government's economic, commercial and social policies
- obligations under the Citizen's Charter initiative, especially the Taxpayer's Charter, Traveller's Charter and

the three charter standard documents which cover the main areas of departmental activity
- deregulation
- EU developments, especially the continuing impact of the Single Market Programme
- the growing complexity of business
- the increasing sophistication of those evading duties, prohibitions and restrictions.

Plans are in place to respond to these requirements, tighten cost control and drive up efficiency and effectiveness by:

- maintaining the capacity to deal with rapid change
- improving the quality of service
- developing further, in a spirit of partnership, relationships with the professional and business community
- increasing the use of audit-based controls which take full account of risk assessment and intelligence
- encouraging an open and participative management style, valuing Customs & Excise staff and ensuring they are better skilled and equipped
- developing an integrated performance management system
- strengthening the link between pay and individual contribution.

Background to pay and grading changes

The Government's policy on Civil Service pay changed significantly in July 1992 when the Chancellor announced a new approach which had the following objectives:

- to make pay more responsive to the market
- to ensure that value for money is obtained from the Civil Service paybill

- to avoid pay increases for the Civil Service which are incompatible with the Government's policies for the economy and public spending
- to deliver high-quality and affordable public services
- to increase transparency in relation to pay costs.

It was against this background that Customs & Excise agreed with ministers that it would take on responsibility for delegated pay bargaining with a view to putting new systems in place by 1 April 1994.

The development of personnel strategy

Customs & Excise started, however, not with pay but with human resource strategy. A major initiative 'Customs and Excise People', which focused on development and performance management, preceded initiatives on pay. Customs & Excise believe that an important first step in the design of effective pay systems is to be clear about the general principles that should guide the development of particular schemes. Customs therefore identified the following key principles:

- Total commitment from senior management is essential.
- Pay schemes should directly support the business needs of the organisation.
- Effective communication procedures must be in place.
- Management of schemes should be delegated as far as possible.
- Paybill modelling and robust control systems should be in place before schemes are introduced.
- Schemes should be fair and open and be supported by effective performance agreements and appraisal systems.
- Schemes should provide rewards for the majority of

staff – not just the outstanding performers. (Poor performers should not receive pay increases.)
- The operation of schemes should be regularly monitored and evaluated.

Applying these principles, Customs & Excise set the following aims and objectives for its pay schemes:

- support departmental business needs
- secure the confidence of staff
- provide a clear link between performance and reward
- be consistent with other aspects of personnel policy (eg performance management and equal opportunities)
- be affordable and lie within the framework set by Government for public sector pay.

These reflected both Customs' views on pay strategy and the main threads of Government requirements on public service pay.

Key changes to pay arrangements

Important issues for resolution in the early stages of the delegation process were union recognition and the procedure for negotiation. The department formally recognised the four unions representing departmental staff, the National Union of Civil and Public Servants (NUCPS), the Association of First Division Civil Servants (FDA), the Civil and Public Services Association (CPSA) and the Institution of Professionals, Managers and Specialists (IPMS). The unions, which have a total membership of 20,700, agreed proposals for handling the negotiations, including single-table bargaining.

The negotiations took place over a period of several months and resulted in agreement on new arrangements to replace the Treasury national pay agreements in June 1994 that had the following main features:

- a new common settlement date of 1 June for all grades (to link performance assessment at the year end [31 March] directly with awards)
- the introduction of two fully performance-related pay schemes
- an overall settlement of 2.6 per cent of which 0.4 per cent covered transition and guarantee costs
- no automatic annual award or increments, but increases dependent on affordability and level of performance, with no awards for poor performers
- withdrawal from the levels surveys carried out by the Office of Manpower Economics (OME) for central Civil Service pay negotiations, and disengagement from the central commitment to make offers within the inter-quartile range identified by the OME's movements research, through retaining a commitment to 'have regard to' those results for the time being
- agreement to develop, in consultation with the unions, new arrangements for the collection and analysis of relevant information – but no formula-driven pay
- transitional guarantees for certain staff moving to new schemes
- a pay agreement with the unions
- provision for monitoring in respect of equal opportunities.

A significant outcome of the negotiations was the signing of a single pay agreement by all four unions. The document provided a framework for new pay schemes and covered important procedural issues such as handling appeals, amendment and termination of the agreement, and arrangements for future pay determination.

The scheme for middle and senior managers has a separate pay range for each grade, with a minimum and maximum and no fixed points in between. All increases in basic pay are performance-related. Staff who perform fully satisfactorily are eligible for an award; the amount is at the discretion of the awarding officer and is consolidated and paid as part of pensionable pay, except where an award takes an individual above the range maximum. In such cases the amount by which the award exceeds the range maximum will be paid as a non-consolidated bonus which will not count towards pension.

The awarding officer takes account of a number of factors in deciding the amount to be paid:

- the extent of achievement towards each objective in a performance agreement
- the importance of each objective
- the loading of the job in terms of volume and complexity of work
- any matters which may have affected achievement but which were outside the job holder's control.

The settlement for executive and clerical staff was designed to take account of the change of settlement date. It also reflected the need for a greater degree of certainty about the amount of performance awards at more junior levels, while also making the extent of progression for a given level of performance dependent on the outcome of the annual negotiation. Under these arrangements the pay schemes for individual grades were replaced by a single fixed spine of approximately 1 to 2 per cent steps so that all grades within the scheme could be positioned on the spine. The values which form the spine remain the same from year to year. All increases in basic pay take the form of progression up the spine and the number of steps is determined by the overall performance achieved (as assessed by a five-box system). The number of steps progressed for each box marking and the level of the maximums and minimums for each grade are subject to annual negotiation with the unions. Performance awards are consolidated up to a set point for a particular box marking. Performance awards above this are by way of non-consolidated and non-pensionable bonuses.

The budget for this scheme in 1994 included elements for transition and guarantee costs and previous incremental progression. An important aspect of this scheme is that staff can directly relate the performance they achieve (as assessed by the five-box system) to the award payable.

Both schemes are subject to rigorous budgetary control.

The new pay arrangements form an important element in the department's performance management system, of which the other key parts are individual performance agreements and effective appraisal procedures.

The lessons learned

The move to delegated pay changed the department's role in the management of pay and allowances fundamentally. The move away from formula-driven pay settlements tied to the inter-quartile range of settlements and from inflexible central schemes has provided a welcome opportunity to put in place pay arrangements that support the business directly by strengthening the link between individual performance and reward.

In their first year, the new systems provided increases in the range 0 per cent (poor performers) to 8 per cent for staff who made an outstanding contribution. An appeals system is in place for resolving disputes. The previous automatic link between the overall level of pay settlement and the revalorisation of attendance-related allowances has been broken, and increases in 1994 were limited to 2 per cent.

CHAPTER SIX

Managing the Paradoxes

Helen Murlis

Throughout this book we have stressed that there are no absolute answers to getting reward policies right. Developing approaches that work typically involves balancing the benefits of particular solutions in a continuously changing environment. From the case-studies, from analysis of the broader economic scene, and from looking at the current pressures on management in both the private and public sectors, we have identified a series of paradoxes that organisations are having to consider.

From the many contributions to this book, the following questions have emerged:

- How can organisations get across the message that they have to do more with fewer resources/less cash to survive?
- If the 'job/career for life' ethic has gone, how do organisations win commitment from employees?
- How can organisations successfully reward learning/skills development and competency acquisition and use when it is the 'bottom line' that ensures survival?
- How can organisations devolve pay decision-making and avoid the problems of pay leap-frogging, pattern bargaining and pay drift?
- What messages are organisations really giving to employees when the better they perform and the more

innovative they are, the fewer jobs there will be?
- How do organisations motivate the 'engine room', the 60 to 80 per cent of employees who form the backbone of most organisations – good, reliable, core staff who don't get the challenging jobs or assignments given to high achievers?
- How do organisations manage pay in an environment where staff on contract or with external contractors are working side by side with 'core' employees, but on different pay and conditions of employment and subject to different pay philosophies?
- What approaches to managing pay relativities can organisations use where roles are flexible and pay is agreed individually?
- How should staff responsible for remuneration policy and practice respond when top management or other stakeholders insist on taking a view of pay that is illiterate in HR/reward management terms?

Although it is not possible to provide absolute answers to these questions, it is worth reflecting on the kind of thinking that is going into current responses. These are summarised below as a contribution to the current pay debate. They reflect the view that work is more than an economic transaction for most people working in developed economies – it is part of the fabric of society, and that by recognising this, organisations can better encourage and manage high performance from the people they employ.

Doing more with less

In the early chapters of this book we describe how, in the private sector, global competition has forced companies to think internationally about every aspect of their business. The same kind of forces are also having some impact on the public sector. Such forces breed employee insecurity, as do the continuing downward pressures on public spending in the Civil Service, local government and the NHS. Motivating fearful and insecure employees is hard, especially when time-honoured approaches to reward, such as protection of purchasing power through annual pay increases into which the cost of living has been factored, are under threat. This is not an area where any employer can pretend that things will get better or that it is only a matter of time before the old order comes round again – it won't.

Successful employers have based their reward strategies on openness about the realities and on gaining the trust of their employees that they will decide intelligently how best to cope with current challenges. The Rover case-study provides an excellent example of how this can be achieved. Throughout the changes of the last few years management has sought to build employee confidence in the future and now, through the 'new deal', the company specifically offers security of employment. In tandem with this, however, the company has successfully changed the nature, size and balance of its workforce through training and development programmes and also through very generous voluntary severance programmes.

Similarly, HM Customs & Excise have responded to the need to deliver further efficiency savings by being very clear about the implications of, for instance, their fundamental expenditure reviews (which will mean cutbacks in staff numbers of about 4,000 from the current level of 26,000), how the new ways of working will be developed, and how voluntary severance will be used as far as possible to achieve the downsizing targets. In a widely dispersed workforce, sophisticated means of communication such as simultaneous live television broadcasts with questions to top management about the implications of change have been used successfully to reinforce the key messages.

As the case-studies show, both organisations are actively rewarding flexibility and the ability to achieve efficiency gains and cost savings by setting values and linked objectives in their performance management processes. This is carried through in the messages given with performance rewards. A similar picture emerges from the Employment Service and the Derby City General Hospital Trust.

Securing commitment when there are no 'jobs for life'

The time when changing jobs several times during a career was taken as a sign of 'unreliability' is long gone. Only in very large and/or very stable organisations does it appear possible to manage a career within a single-employer environment. Even then this may not be desirable for either party. People who stay in a single environment can become institutionalised and narrow in their perspectives and be more resistant to change. Those who move almost inevitably acquire a broader perspective about work. They see different work cultures and styles of management as well as approaches to motivating staff and managing rewards. The concept of the 'portfolio career' has certainly taken root among graduates and professionals who now typically seek to build up a set of complementary experiences in different environments as part of their personal career management process.

But in parallel with employees who choose to move and who have 'bought in' to a more fluid career pattern, there are those who are either stuck in a stagnant job market or do not see the value of movement because they hold a more 'traditional' outlook on loyalty. The commitment of both has to be managed and rewarded.

For these groups the answer lies in building in opportunities for development. This is where competencies come in and where rewards for competency acquisition and use, often within the framework of performance management, can play their part. Well designed competency frameworks provide very powerful messages and a new language around both proficient and excellent performance. They can also provide the basis on which people can take ownership of their development – for which they can be rewarded. This approach has been adopted in most of the case-studies covered in this book. Organisations such as ICL, Mercury, the Derby City General Hospital Trust, the Employment Service and HM Customs & Excise have used competencies, and are continuing to develop the way they use them, to provide increasing clarity about what the components of successful performance look like.

Rewarding both input and output

In the early 1990s there was a great deal of talk about competency-based pay. The idea captured the imagination of top management in many large organisations with the appreciation that it was not just what people did that mattered, but also how they behaved. Paying for contribution in terms of the competencies displayed and the skills acquired suddenly became very fashionable. The appeal of this also grew in the face of some disillusionment with reward systems based purely on the achievement of personal objectives cascaded from business plans (which anyway cannot always be parcelled out neatly into 'bite-sized chunks' in all areas of an organisation).

For the professions – eg lawyers, doctors, nurses – or indeed for any job where qualitative factors matter more in defining performance than concrete results, payment for inputs and personal contribution has to be a sensible approach; but it is not a universal panacea. Companies, like Mercury and First Direct, that have based their reward policies on contribution management have some pretty hard and measurable business targets in place, where their achievement is within the control of individuals or teams, and where they best define performance. In many organisations, so-called mixed models of performance management have grown up. These approaches balance the acquisition and use of competencies and skills with the achievement of business objectives set against agreed performance measures. This is the approach, for instance, in HM Customs & Excise where hard revenue targets have to be met, but where changes in behaviour have actively been sought in terms of competency development to enable staff to operate effectively in a more empowered environment.

Devolution and the avoidance of leap-frogging and pay drift

We have recorded earlier in this book the seemingly inexorable trend towards decentralising pay management and devolving pay decisions as close as possible to the point where they are implemented. This started in the private sector in the 1980s and is proceeding apace in the public sector in the 1990s. Of course, the centralised pay bargaining we all grew up with had appeared in the first place for some very powerful economic reasons. At a time when the economy was expanding, when union power was strong and growing, when there remained only a hard core of unemployed, and where the majority of employers had poor pay negotiating skills, then centralised agreements and pay bargaining seemed an entirely proper means of providing stability. It certainly enabled bodies like the Engineering Employers' Federation to contain the problem of pattern bargaining and pay leap-frogging that had dogged the industry previously and dented its world competitiveness – even if it did give rise to the pay drift which so exercised the Donovan Commission in 1968.

Nowadays centralised pay management sits ill with the way in which people are managed and with policies to devolve control to the line. The reality is that centralised pay policies (or indeed performance management systems) are rarely 'owned' by those who apply them.

However, organisations can't switch from centralised to decentralised policies overnight. Judgements have to be made about those things which it is cost-effective to retain centrally. Judgements also have to be made about where consistency across an organisation matters and where it is needed to enable employee mobility and sustain common values. Frameworks have to be built to ensure that sensible financial controls exist and through which devolution can be managed and controlled locally. So it is no accident, for example, that the Civil Service is not currently seeking to make changes to its central pension scheme; or that, while the Treasury is keen to see locally-determined pay systems in the departments and agencies that have taken, or will take, delegated responsibility for pay, it is keeping a very close eye on negotiating briefs and paybill models to ensure that good practice and effective cost controls will be in place in the new environment. And senior management pay remains centralised to a significant degree and still subject to pay review body recommendations. It is, after all, only following the example of companies like ICL and other major employers whose reward and financial control practices it has scrutinised in the last few years as policies have evolved. And much has been done, too, to spread the word about the importance of building management capability to take effective pay decisions in a devolved environment. Early successes include the CAA as well as a range of large agencies and non-departmental public bodies.

All of this decentralisation, some would argue, has not yet been properly tested. In an environment where unemployment persists, where there are few skill shortages and where there is less mobility in the face of continuing insecurity, the pre-conditions for leap-frogging are simply not there.

When the test comes, much will depend on the quality of the policies that have been put in place, the extent to which employers resort to throwing money at short-term recruitment or retention problems, and by how much the trade unions go for short-term-gain on the pay front. Many would argue, however, that the quality and nature of employee relations is now fundamentally different and that pattern bargaining was a product of a confrontational and low-trust environment that has now largely disappeared; we shall see.

The better you perform and the more innovative you are, the fewer jobs there will be

There is a story sometimes told in personnel circles that in the factory of the future there will be only one highly rewarded person and a dog. The person will be there to monitor the working of the whole place and the dog will be there to keep him or her company and to stop a human being from touching the machines. Is this the ultimate result of upskilling the workforce? There are certainly some very tough messages for jobs, and therefore for rewards, in the push for lean and innovative organisations. Continued downsizing through early retirements and redundancies have, however well managed, left their scars. Yet companies like Rover have pushed out the frontiers of productivity and improved employee morale and rewards in precisely this environment.

They have achieved this by talking to their employees about secure employment for all who perform well and work with new values, and about rewarding the acquisition and use of new skills which they need continually to develop. They have done this on the basis of long-term investment in development of all their people as well as by enhancing management skills. These messages have been carried forward in 'new' organisations such as Mercury and First Direct, where the lessons from their parent companies (Cable and Wireless and Midland Bank respectively) have informed policy development in new 'green field' sites.

Motivating the engine room

Much of the thinking that went into the performance-related pay schemes of the 1980s centred on rewarding key players and ensuring that high performance gained significant rewards. At board level and for senior management, this approach seems self-evident. It has, however, proved hard to sustain lower down organisations. Where performance pay budgets have been tight the range of performance rewards on offer has not been very wide. In these circumstances a very few high performers will get increases, perhaps through one-off non-consolidated bonuses, of close to 10 per cent. For the 'fully acceptable' group – the 70 to 80 per cent of people with middle performance ratings – survey and other pay research evidence suggests that the increases available have typically been nearer 3 to 5 per cent, ie at around the general movement in earnings, or what they might have expected anyway.

Awards have certainly been less than in the days when a cost of living adjustment went with a guaranteed service-related increment of 2 to 3 per cent in many cases. It is not surprising, therefore, to find that trying to motivate the average-performing employee with the promise of significant payments has simply proved impossible, and appears to be a bad case of 'who is kidding whom?'

You could deduce from this (and some have done so) that, on the basis of the payments actually made, performance-related pay 'isn't working' and is just divisive and demotivating. Yet this is not the evidence from any of our case-studies. From the attitude surveys conducted by ICL, employee consultation within Mercury, and similar studies in the other organisations we have looked at, it is clear that motivating the 'engine room' has been only partly viewed as a pay issue. While recognising that good, reliable 'core' performance and performance improvement were critical components of business success, achieving this has come through quality initiatives, continuing development programmes and, most importantly, through making all employees feel much more valued and able to contribute to their full potential. Behind this lies a much more empowered model of the employment relationship and a view that for the majority of employees pay should be used to support rather than lead policy change. Much of the work currently going on in the area of performance rewards is about fine-tuning current practice and making sure that the pay messages are congruent with the other messages being given to employees. In particular, work is needed to iron out the conflicts between continuous performance management and annual performance marking.

Where teamwork matters, then rewarding team contribution either through team rewards or, more commonly, by defining teamworking competencies and focusing on them in terms of performance management, is being developed. And there is the interesting case of the air traffic controllers at the CAA where focusing on producing as little variation as possible against strict performance requirements and eschewing performance-related pay has proved the most sensible policy to adopt.

Rewarding permanent staff working alongside an 'outsourced' workforce

An important component of change in many organisations is disinvestment activities that are no longer deemed to be 'core'. Services and activities have been put out on contract: many IT departments, for instance, are now run on a 'facilities management' basis with employees of a major supplier of such services working alongside permanent staff. Market testing and compulsory competitive tendering have accelerated the process in the public sector. There is every indication that we are moving in some areas towards the creation of 'virtual organisations' brought together through temporary strategic alliances, much in the way that cinema films have been made, or complex construction projects run. For more traditional organisations this approach will inevitably produce tensions and some conflicts on the employment front.

Different workforces employed under different contracts representing different management values will inevitably talk to each other and compare notes and show concern if the difference in their treatment seems too large. We are at the beginning of learning how to manage the issues that will emerge. The emphasis so far has been on skilful contract negotiation and management, and on planning for the effects of the transfer of undertakings legislation (TUPE) on employment conditions. But as workforces are transferred in larger numbers, while continuing to work on site with their 'old' colleagues, competing pay strategies are bound to come into play.

The lessons about managing all this are likely to come from organisations that take a long-term interest in the employment and the operating policies of their suppliers. Companies like Marks & Spencer which enforce strict standards are likely to become role models for making these new arrangements work effectively.

Managing pay relativities where roles are flexible and pay is individual

For most of our case-studies, finely graded pay structures containing carefully defined, fixed jobs are a thing of the past. Mercury and First Direct never had them to start with. The traditional world of job evaluation and the strict control of conformity was not for them. For these new organisations, and for many more 'traditional' organisations such as the CAA, the focus has been on creating flexibility and fostering the development of flexible roles either within job families or professional communities, as in the case of ICL, or indeed individually. Yet organisations still have to measure and manage pay relativities by tracking salary market levels and by rewarding individuals and groups accordingly. They still have to explain and justify why one role is paid more than another, as well as the factors in terms of performance, skill level or market behaviour, which have influenced pay decisions. There is also equal-value legislation to respect, and account to be taken of the deeply held belief that pay should be 'fair'.

In this environment, and as the 1996 CBI/Hay survey[1] found, the majority of organisations are not abandoning job evaluation, but they are jettisoning old, cumbersome approaches and procedures and learning to use the new approaches. Job family models, which reflect the levels at which work is done in a specific area, the key elements of work and the corresponding competencies are, for example, often underpinned by some form of measurement of the size of each level – both to inform understanding of the 'shape' of the family and to assist with matching the levels to the market data being used.

Both for job families and for individual roles, templates and profiles are being produced, jointly with employees, which help to define what is required, while not constraining flexibility when it is needed. These new approaches enable organisations better to manage diversity while providing employees with the clarity they need over what is expected of them. Role templates are used not just for managing and measuring relativities, but also for recruitment, career planning and performance management.

Such approaches are often implemented within so-called 'broad-banded' pay structures – containing roles of different sizes and pay ranges that can be up to 200 per cent or more wide. Use of these is growing in the private sector, and the public sector too is looking hard at the options. Operating pay policies in this environment has provided much more flexibility, but it has also made some strong demands on organisations.

In summary, theses new approaches require:

- well developed career management programmes that enable employees to see how they can manage their own progression in an environment where promotion is rarer and more significant when it happens, and when building experience in different roles is the way to progress
- well designed and implemented performance management processes that often embrace the use of competencies and so support development, as well as the achievement of objectives, and which link credibly to performance-related pay progression and other variable pay schemes
- a line management skilled in interpreting market data, in making local pay decisions and in operating and communicating the policies needed for this new environment
- well validated salary market 'anchors' for the new roles which managers can review and use as background for pay budgeting and pay progression decisions
- strong, locally-based financial control and modelling systems to support decision-making and help ensure the prevention of pay drift.

Building top management appreciation of the background to reward strategy development

We are still living largely with a generation of senior managers whose appreciation of the influences on pay, and the way in which pay decisions need to be integrated with other people management issues, is far from complete. Many chief executives have risen through the financial or marketing route, and acquiring an understanding of the issues discussed in this book has not been central to their achievement of a senior executive role. At a time when they might have picked up the basics, ten or more years ago, the world of reward practice was different anyway. Even those who passed through personnel on their way up may remember a very different environment from that being created in leading organisations today. Yet this group is now being asked to decide on pay issues and allocate paybill costs against a set of philosophies they may understand only partially. Some of them take a lot of briefing and influencing to help them understand the issues at stake. Others are still too prone to looking for reward strategies that accord with an understanding based on partial information from the media and from others in their peer group of professional contacts, which may be a long way from reality.

Pay is still in some places a 'fashion' business, and change is often sought much faster than can sensibly be managed. As we have shown in Chapter 3, there are plenty of theories to choose from – and not all are helpful undiluted.

Where there is a lack of pay literacy at senior levels, and where major changes are being sought, a range of strategies exists to help ensure that well-informed decisions eventually win the day:

- surveying employee attitudes on what motivates people and how they feel about current policies; and presenting

the evidence on the basis that if you want to test out how well a reward strategy is working, find out from those to whom it applies
- providing summaries of benchmark company practice and the influences behind their reward strategy decisions
- organising briefings and workshops designed to build understanding of current pay practice and thinking, and relating these to individual organisational issues, ahead of the time when real decisions have to be taken
- providing individual discussions on specific issues to fill out understanding.

Any or all of these have been used in our case-studies.

Of course, many of the new generation of managers currently reaching senior positions view pay very differently. They have undergone more development, take a stronger interest in the motivation of their people and have more 'hands on' experience of managing the pay and performance issues covered in this book. This group will not be content with the old orthodoxies at all. They will be looking for creativity, they will expect IT systems to support more effective processes, and they will want to 'own' pay as part of the day-to-day toolkit of managing their team or their organisation. They are perhaps at the other side of the crossroads described in this book and their relationships with the HR professionals who develop reward strategies will be fundamentally different.

REFERENCES

1 CBI/Hay Management Consultants (1996) *Trends in Pay and Benefits Systems.*
2 CBI/Towers Perrin (1992) *The Benefits Package of the Future.*
3 Nickell, S. J. (1995) *The Performance of Companies.* Oxford, Blackwell.
4 Marsden, D. and Richardson, R. (1994) 'Performing for pay? The effects of merit pay on motivation in the British public service'. *British Journal of Industrial Relations.* June, pp. 243–61.
5 Thompson, M. (1992) *Performance-Related Pay: The employer experience.* IMS, University of Sussex.
6 Fernie, S., Metcalf. D. and Woodland, S. (1994) 'What has human resource management achieved in the workplace?' *Employment Policy Institute Economic Report*, 8, 3.
7 Hamel, G. and Prahalad, C. K. (1994) *Competing for the Future.* Boston, Harvard Business School Press.

Index

allowances to improve flexibility 9
annual increments to pay 15, 27–8, 34, 104, 108, 135, 140, 146
   large 26–7
appraisal system(s) *see* performance appraisal system
Australia, comparison with 31

Bell Canada Enterprises 72
benefits 14, 16, 19–20, 22, 69, 72, 76–8, 109, 123
   choice in/of 19, 76-8
   packages with pay 24, 67, 69, 76–8, 114
   see also flexible benefits
BMW 87, 95
bonuses 14, 16, 84–5, 91, 93, 136, 146
   non-consolidated, non-pensionable 16, 136, 137, 146
Britain as major trading nation 2
   labour costs comparison *see* labour costs, international comparisons of
   share of world trade 2–3
British Aerospace 88
British Leyland *see* Rover
British Quality Foundation, the 91
broadbanding 14, 17, 150
BT (British Telecommunications plc) 10, 72, 74
business agenda *see* organisational business agenda
business objectives *see* organisational objectives/goals
business strategy *see* organisational strategy

CAA *see* Civil Aviation Authority
Cable and Wireless 72, 146
career development of individual employees 18, 32, 79, 82, 86–7, 92, 94–5, 101, 116, 126, 150
case-studies 9, 10–11, 12, 13, 14, 17, 22, 33, 57, 61, 62–96, 105–137, 138, 140–42, 147, 149, 152
CBI (the Confederation of British Industries) 17, 18, 19, 20, 29, 149
change, in organisational structure *see* organisational structure
  in working practices 9, 20, 22, 23, 28, 64, 107, 122
  pay as the agent of 14, 20
China, comparison with 3
Citizen's Charter, the 11, 99, 131
Civil Aviation Authority (CAA), the 9, 11, 98, 144, 147, 149
collective bargaining/negotiation 25, 27, 31, 35, 58, 64, 92, 106, 112, 134–5, 143
communications within organisations 9, 13, 14, 18, 20–22, 64, 140
  methods and media 20-22
company cost structures *see* organisational cost structures
company culture *see* organisational culture/mission/values
company strategy *see* organisational strategy
comparability in/of pay 25, 27–30, 35, 41, 43
competency-based management 8, 33–4, 142, 150
competency-based vacancy filling 9, 18, 36, 116, 118
competency-related pay 14, 18, 22, 101, 142
Confederation of British Industries *see* CBI
containment of public expenditure 8
contracting out 12, 31, 97, 148
  see also outsourcing of services
contract of employment, open-ended 13
  traditional 12
  see also psychological contract
cost-cutting 8, 30, 63, 126, 141

cost of living increase(s) 25, 27–8, 146
counselling 78
customer-orientation 12, 18, 23, 32, 35, 36, 37, 52, 78, 80, 88-9, 96, 102
Customs and Excise *see* HM Customs & Excise

debt 26
decentralisation of pay bargaining/awards 8, 28, 31–2, 98, 102–5, 143–4
decisions about pay 1
deferred compensation model 47–8
delayering 16, 17, 32, 95, 118, 123
demanning *see* downsizing
demotivation 30, 44, 147
Derby City General Hospital Trust 10–11, 18, 22, 98, 102, 124–30, 141, 142
deregulation 11, 41, 132
devaluation of national currency 6
DHL Worldwide Express 59
disaffection among employees 42
dismissal 47
Donovan Commission/Report, the 57–8, 144
downsizing 12, 37, 140, 145

earnings, national 6–7
economic cycles 40
economic growth in Britain, recovering 40
  slowing 5–6
efficiency, increased business 8, 12, 23
efficiency wage hypothesis, the 43
employee commitment 12, 13, 32, 35, 138, 141–2
employee development *see* training and development of employees
employment costs *see* labour costs
Employment Service, the 9, 11, 20, 98, 114–24, 141, 142
  Jobcentres 115

empowerment of employees 5, 16, 75, 143, 147
enterprise culture 5
equal opportunities/value legislation 37, 149
ESOPs 53
exports 2, 26

'feel good' factor *see* pay and the 'feel good' factor
financial strategy 1
First Direct Bank 10–11, 16, 18, 22, 78–87, 142, 146, 149
flexible benefits 14, 18–20
flexible pay 12, 14, 17
   see also variable pay
flexible working practices 16, 30, 31, 42, 57, 89, 124, 126, 141, 149
foreign investment *see* investment from abroad
France, comparison with 3, 4

gainsharing plans 15
Germany, comparison with 3, 4, 7–8, 31
globalisation of markets 4–5
goal-setting 51

Hay Management Consultants 17, 18, 19, 120, 149
HM Customs & Excise 11, 16, 98, 102, 130–37, 140, 142
HMSO (Her Majesty's Stationery Office) 104
home ownership 26, 27
Honda 88, 90, 95
Hong Kong, comparison with 2–3
Hong Kong and Shanghai Banking Corporation 79
house purchases *see* home ownership
HRM *see* personnel (HRM) function
human resource strategy *see* personnel policy/strategy

IBM 63
ICL plc 10–11, 13, 18, 19–20, 21–2, 62–72, 142, 144, 147, 149
imports 2
   of manufactured goods 2

incentive schemes/systems 14, 33, 45, 51–3
  see also performance-related pay, individualised
India, comparison with 3
individual merit pay *see* performance-related pay, individualised
industrial action 120
industrial relations, difficult/poor 10, 58, 113
industrial tribunals, awards by 24
inflation 2, 6, 24, 26, 58, 103
  effect on property values 26
  increasing/rising 26
  in retail prices 40–41, 42
  in wages 40, 42
  low 25–6, 29, 40, 113
  relationship to pay 24–6, 103
  relationship to productivity 27
  Treasury targets for 40
inflexible working practices 10
Institute of Employment Studies, the 15
Institute of Manpower Studies *see* Institute of Employment Studies, the
interest rates 30
investment from abroad 3–4
investment in the community 5
investment per employee 7
Investors in People initiative, the 33
IPD (the Institute of Personnel and Development) 59

Japan, comparison with 2, 3, 4, 7–8, 10, 16, 31, 88
job evaluation 22, 35, 58, 64, 69, 71, 74, 117–18, 121, 149
  Treasury systems for 117, 121
job families 71–2, 86–7, 149
job satisfaction 48–9, 126

labour costs 38, 39, 125
  British 4, 6–7

international comparisons of 4, 6, 38
low/lower 4
rising 6
labour market, British 39, 40, 41, 42, 60, 99, 115
   competition and competitiveness in 39, 41, 42–5, 115
   internal 45, 47–8
   international 4, 37
   national comparisons 4
learning theory 49–50
London Business School, the 64

macro-economic policy, constraints/influences on 39, 98–9
   Governmental 7
   organisational 39–42
Malaysia, comparison with 3
management 1, 25, 32, 33, 34, 36, 41, 45–6, 83, 110
   line 25, 59, 74–5, 78, 94, 121–3, 127, 150
   style(s) of 13, 67, 88, 129–30, 132
   theory 39
   see also performance management
Management Centre Europe (consultancy) 60
marketing strategy 1
market testing 31, 97
Marks & Spencer 148
Mercury Communications 10, 19, 72–8, 142, 146, 147, 149
merit pay schemes *see* performance-related pay, individualised
Midland Bank 78–9, 82, 84, 146
minimum wage, national 29
motivation of the workforce 9, 15, 17, 33, 36, 48–51, 54, 57, 67, 81, 84, 92, 95, 139, 140, 146–7, 152
   pay as agent for 32, 48–9, 55
motivation theories 48–51, 60
   expectancy theory 50–51, 54
   individual need theory 48–9
   orientations theory 49

reinforcement theory/behaviour modification theory 49–50
multiskilling 12, 16, 124

national agreements on pay 31, 119
'new pay' issues 14
NHS (the National Health Service) 8, 31, 98, 99, 100, 104, 125, 128, 140

organisational business agenda 1–23, 35
    influences on 2–13
organisational cost structures 40
organisational culture/mission/values 1, 15, 23, 34, 35, 37, 55, 56, 60, 64, 80–81, 90–91, 92, 96, 130
organisational objectives/goals 11, 13, 19, 22, 25, 57, 59, 64, 66, 82, 101, 105, 130, 141, 143
organisational strategy 11, 27, 33, 63, 90–91, 96, 104, 105
organisational structure, changes in 9, 13, 32, 34, 46, 91, 96, 107
    flat/flatter 13, 17, 32, 74
outsourcing of services 29, 37, 148
overtime pay 14

Pacific rim nations, comparison with 38
parity issues 32
partnerships, strategic 37
part-time working, growth of 29
pay, 'administered' 25
    as a 'hygiene' factor 48–9
    comparability in/of *see* comparability in/of pay
    competency-related *see* competency-related pay
    flexibility in *see* flexible pay
    low 28-9
    overtime *see* overtime pay
    profit-related *see* profit-related pay scheme(s)
    shift *see* shift pay

'strategic' 25, 33–4; *see also* pay policy
systems of *see* pay systems
variable *see* variable pay
pay and the 'feel good' factor 25, 30
pay cut(s) 28, 44
pay delegation 102–5, 134–7
pay freeze 28, 44
pay increases 15, 26–30
see also annual increments to pay
payment by results (PBR) 46
pay policy, Governmental 27, 97, 99, 101, 112, 113, 134
influences on organisational 1, 13, 14, 15, 39, 43, 109–11, 134, 142–3, 148
pay review bodies 9, 28, 103, 104, 124, 144
pay systems 14–20, 23, 31, 33, 34–6, 37, 46, 55, 74, 97–105, 110, 114, 127, 129–30, 134–7, 148
'fit for purpose' 8, 31, 99
pay thresholds 28
people as organisational asset 5
people management issues 24, 25, 34-5, 117
performance appraisal/measurement/review 9, 15, 21–2, 30, 35–6, 46, 52, 54, 64, 66, 68–70, 75-6, 82, 83–4, 103, 111, 116, 117–18, 133, 137
'balanced scorecard' measurement 33, 117, 136
performance management 18, 30, 33, 34, 36, 64–7, 72, 75, 79, 82–4, 116, 133–4, 137, 141–4, 150, 152
performance-related pay (PRP), 'failures' of 24, 147
individualised 8, 14, 15, 16, 46, 52–3, 65, 73–4, 93, 100, 101, 103, 136, 150
schemes for 9, 13–14, 15, 16, 18, 35–6, 57, 64–72, 84–5, 93–4, 98, 100–03, 109, 111–12, 117–19, 122–3, 128, 130, 135–7, 146, 147, 150
personal development *see* career development of individual employees
personnel (HRM) function 59-61, 73, 74, 98, 104, 117, 139
personnel policy/strategy 1, 11, 22, 32, 33, 34, 59, 61, 63,

82–4, 105, 126, 133–4
  pay as part of 1, 24
piece rates/piecework 35, 58, 91
'portfolio career/working' 31, 141
principal agent theory 45–8, 51, 53–4
privatisation 31
problem-solving 5, 52
production strategy 1
productivity, growth/increase in 8, 12, 28, 30, 41–2, 53, 63, 89, 145
  in manufacturing 6, 10
  national 7
  per employee 7-8, 40, 47, 63, 85
profit-related pay scheme(s) 17, 93
profit sharing 14, 53
psychological contract, the 13, 32, 36, 55, 92

quality issues 12, 23, 30, 35, 82, 102, 126
questionnaire(s) 22, 121, 127–8

recession, the 30, 40, 41, 63, 98
remuneration approach/strategy 1, 13, 14, 15, 17, 18, 22, 33, 34, 36, 37, 42, 49–50, 54, 57–8, 59, 60, 61, 64–71, 75, 78, 79, 81–7, 91–4, 96, 98, 105, 115, 121, 124, 125–8, 137, 138–9, 142–3, 151–2
research and development 12, 127–8
resourcing, tightening up on 28
retail price index, reference to 28, 64
reward approach/management/strategy *see* remuneration approach/strategy
role profile(s) 22, 83, 149–50
Rover Group 10, 13, 17, 22, 87–96, 140, 145

share options 19
share plans/schemes 14, 17
shift pay 14, 109

Singapore, comparison with 2–3
skills, development/acquisition of 15, 18, 30, 32, 35, 44, 50, 62, 71–2, 90, 138, 141–3, 145–6
   shortages of 30
   specific and general 44
'social contract(s)' 27
South Korea, comparison with 2–3
Spain, comparison with 3
survey(s) on pay 17, 18
Sweden, comparison with 4, 31

Taiwan, comparison with 2–3
tax relief 17
tax system, the 17
teamworking 12, 13, 14, 16, 18, 33, 35, 101, 103, 147
technological change(s) 4
temporary work 31
Thailand, comparison with 3
time rates 34
total quality concepts 12, 67, 88, 90–91
Towers Perrin (consultants) 19, 20, 61
TQM *see* total quality concepts
trade imbalance(s) 2
trade union involvement 20, 25, 31–2, 42, 64–5, 69, 73, 88, 93, 102, 104, 106, 108, 110–12, 117, 120, 124, 129, 134–5, 137, 143, 145
Trade Union Reform and Employee Rights Act 1993 58
training and development of employees 13, 17, 18, 29, 33, 44, 66, 82, 101, 140
transfer of undertakings 148

UK *see* Britain
unemployment rate in Britain 6, 40, 115
unions and unionisation *see* trade union involvement
university course/degree collaboration 95
USA, comparison with 3, 4, 7–8

variable pay 14–17
VAT and its implications 11, 131

wage councils 28, 29, 58
wage cut, wage freeze *see* pay cut(s); pay freeze
wage/price spiral 31, 40
waste-cutting 12
wealth 27, 98
world economic growth 2
world trade 2
   changes in 2